Leadership Enrichment and Development

This book shares the LEAD (Leadership Enrichment and Development) method, a framework for supporting and facilitating leadership identity development for women in higher education. Guided by feminist group processes and relational learning, the chapters in this volume illustrate the impacts of self- and peer mentorship on the authors. Part lived experience, part reflection on scholarship on women's leadership development, this book has implications for those in leadership development settings across professional sectors and career trajectories, offering strategies, implications, and insights for those developing or seeking to learn about peer mentoring programming for women faculty. Women faculty, leadership development coaches, faculty development leaders, directors of centers for teaching excellence, program leaders focused on girls' and women's leader development, and students and scholars interested in women's leadership development in higher education will find this volume of interest. While LEAD's context is higher education, the volume offers valuable application to other professional settings where women work, lead, and thrive.

Gail Simpson Cahill is a Department Chair and an Associate Professor of Special Education at Lesley University in Cambridge, MA, USA. Dr. Cahill teaches courses in seminar and special education. Dr. Cahill has taught various grades in PreK-12 schools and held several administrative positions in school systems.

Diana C. Direiter is the Dean of Faculty and an Associate Professor of Psychology at Lesley University in Cambridge, MA, USA, and a Licensed Clinical Psychologist. She is a founding member and co-facilitator of Leadership Enrichment and Development (LEAD).

Amy Rutstein-Riley is the Dean of the Graduate School of Leadership and Change and Director of the PhD Program in Leadership and Change at Antioch University, USA. Dr. Rutstein-Riley is the founder of The Girlhood Project and a founding member and co-facilitator of Leadership Enrichment and Development (LEAD).

Stephanie A. Spadorcia is the Vice-Provost of Education and an Associate Professor of Special Education and Literacy at Lesley University in Cambridge, MA, USA. Dr. Spadorcia is a founding member and co-facilitator of Leadership Enrichment and Development (LEAD). Her teaching and research focus on literacy instruction for children with disabilities.

Routledge Studies in Leadership Research

27. **Toxic Leadership**
    Research and Cases
    Steven Walker and Daryl Watkins

28. **Leadership Styles and Job Performance**
    The Impact of Fake Leadership on Organizational Reliability
    Agnieszka Bieńkowska and Katarzyna Tworek

29. **Digital Leadership**
    Evidence from Theory and Practice
    Ahmad M. Salih

30. **Charismatic Leadership in Organizations**
    A Critique of Texts
    Iga Maria Lehman

31. **Subversion, Power and Hierarchy in Organisations and Society**
    Carnivalesque Leadership
    Jo Trevenna

32. **Leadership Enrichment and Development**
    Peer and Self-Mentoring Women in Higher Education
    Edited by Gail Simpson Cahill, Diana C. Direiter, Amy Rutstein-Riley and Stephanie A. Spadorcia

For more information about this series please visit: https://www.routledge.com/Routledge-Studies-in-Leadership-Research/book-series/RSLR

Leadership Enrichment and Development

Peer and Self-Mentoring Women in Higher Education

Edited by Gail Simpson Cahill, Diana C. Direiter, Amy Rutstein-Riley and Stephanie A. Spadorcia

Routledge
Taylor & Francis Group
NEW YORK AND LONDON

First published 2025
by Routledge
605 Third Avenue, New York, NY 10158

and by Routledge
4 Park Square, Milton Park, Abingdon, Oxon, OX14 4RN

Routledge is an imprint of the Taylor & Francis Group, an informa business

ISBN: 978-0-367-47839-1 (hbk)
ISBN: 978-0-367-52257-5 (pbk)
ISBN: 978-1-003-05720-8 (ebk)

DOI: 10.4324/9781003057208

Typeset in Times New Roman
by Apex CoVantage, LLC

This book is dedicated to all the women – known and unknown – who have worked and continue to work to shatter the glass ceilings on behalf of us all.

Contents

Contributors

Gail Simpson Cahill is Department Chair and Associate Professor of Special Education at Lesley University in Cambridge, MA, USA. Dr. Cahill teaches courses in seminar and special education. Dr. Cahill has taught various grades in PreK-12 schools and held several administrative positions in school systems.

Diana C. Direiter is the Dean of Faculty and Associate Professor of Psychology at Lesley University in Cambridge, MA, USA, and Licensed Clinical Psychologist. She is a founding member and co-facilitator of *Leadership Enrichment and Development (LEAD)*.

Barbara Govendo is Professor Emerita of Special Education at Lesley University in Cambridge, MA, USA. Dr. Govendo has experience teaching and supervising educators. She has consulted with over 100 schools in New England and New Mexico. Dr. Govendo is a past president of the Massachusetts Council for Learning Disabilities.

Jana Roberts is Associate Director of the Leadership Studies doctoral program at Trevecca Nazarene University in Nashville, TN, USA. Dr. Roberts served as the Equal Opportunity Officer for the Missouri State University system. Her research interests include leadership identity development, mentorship, and institutional effectiveness.

Robin L. Roth is Professor Emerita of Sociology and Social Policy at Lesley University, Cambridge, MA, USA. Dr. Roth held positions of academic leadership, including dean of the undergraduate college. Her research and teaching are in the areas of social policy, inequality, and gender.

Amy Rutstein-Riley is Dean of the Graduate School of Leadership and Change and Director of the PhD Program of Leadership and Change at Antioch University, USA. Dr. Rutstein-Riley is the founder of *The Girlhood Project* and a founding member and co-facilitator of *Leadership Enrichment and Development (LEAD)*.

Stephanie A. Spadorcia is the Vice-Provost of Education and an Associate Professor of Special Education and Literacy at Lesley University in Cambridge, MA, USA. Dr. Spadorcia is a founding member and co-facilitator of *Leadership Enrichment and Development (LEAD)*. Her teaching and research focus on literacy instruction for children with disabilities.

Barbara Steckel is a retired professor of Language and Literacy at Lesley University, Cambridge, MA, USA. Dr. Steckel served as president of the Massachusetts Reading Association and The Massachusetts Association of College and University Reading Educators. Barbara focuses on the leadership role of literacy coaches and professional development for teachers.

Preface

This volume was several years in the making, beginning in 2015. Since that time, many historical events have occurred to change our lives – COVID-19 probably being the most vivid. During this decade, our individual lives as women changed in expected and unexpected ways as we navigated joy, growth, loss and grief, marriage, childbirth and childrearing, divorce, health challenges, and the beauty and complexities of aging.

Our institutional context has changed as well. We, who all identify as she/her, have changed our roles at the university, with some members retiring and others leaving. One truism has remained: Over the last ten years, each member grew in countless ways, in part shaped by LEAD and in turn shaping the LEAD experience.

The local and higher educational contexts have also changed over the life of this group. Collectively, we have worked for several presidents, faced budgetary realities, and witnessed the reorganization of university structures; that is, we have collectively been involved with the institutional realities that are part of the context of this narrative because our group was produced and shaped within an individual college setting over almost a decade. The differences among institutional priorities exist, but they do not exist in a vacuum and are shaped by the larger social and political contexts of higher education as an institution.

The chapters contained in this volume illustrate the experiences of our LEAD (Leadership Enrichment and Development) group members. The chapters were developed in our co-constructed meetings as we leaned into each other for advice, support, and problem-solving. The topics in this volume emerged as we puzzled through the personal, social, and political realities of our lives as women faculty. Our relationships, relational learning, and approach to peer mentorship grew in purpose and significance.

We are grateful for the initial material support provided by the Office of the Provost at Lesley University to form the LEAD group and continue its funding over several years, and we are grateful for the clarity of commitment to the development of women faculty at our university. The impact of the university administrators to support LEAD-ers proved to have a far greater impact on their leadership journey than attendance or membership in any other organization and should be highlighted as a critical outcome of our group and one that can be applied at other institutions.

Acknowledgments

The editors would like to thank our families and loved ones for providing us with a solid foundation from which to work.

Thank you to our children and grandchildren, who continually gave us space and time to do this work and great stories to share along the way. Our relationships with you were always at the center of our hearts.

Thank you to the mentors, sponsors, friends, and colleagues who have pushed and pulled us through our developmental journeys. A special thank you to the former Provost of Lesley University, Dr. Selase Williams, who championed LEAD with funding for our initial launch and for many subsequent years.

Thank you to our current and former colleagues who participated in LEAD over the years and continued to push us to do better, to challenge our assumptions, and to grow as individual leaders engaged in relational leadership practices. Special gratitude goes to Dr. Marion Nesbit, whose unflagging encouragement and cheerleading for this project were deeply appreciated.

Finally, we want to acknowledge our many students who have touched our lives in and out of the university classroom. They have continually pushed us to think in new and innovative ways, to work towards greater inclusion and opportunity, and to use our individual and collective power to create space for the women coming next. Mentorship, sponsorship, and relationships have fostered our growth in LEAD, and we believe these strategies will do the same for those moving on the same or similar developmental paths.

1 Invitation to LEAD

Amy Rutstein-Riley, Diana C. Direiter, and Stephanie A. Spadorcia

Invitation to LEAD: Forming a Women's Peer and Self-Mentoring Group

You might be reading this book and contemplating your own role in leadership in higher education. You are either in a leadership role or moving toward one. You are looking for mentors and support as you navigate the waters of making not only the necessary career moves but also a development plan to support this career move. If you are like us, you may be noticing pockets of women in leadership positions but not enough mentors available to support your own development. Colorado Women's College 2013 report Benchmarking Women Leadership in Higher Education (Lennon, 2012) highlights the "higher the fewer" paradigm – where the higher the rank and leadership positions are in higher education, the fewer women there are in those positions, despite the fact that women have earned more than 50% of earned doctorates since 2006 (Pasque & Simpson, 2013). This results in fewer mentors available to support to continuously expand the bench.

In 2015, the editors of this book were in the early stages of their own leadership development. We found ourselves in leadership positions, grappling with difficult situations with administration, and other faculty while also feeling the need for leadership development. We were at a university that had a history of women in leadership positions and providing opportunities for leadership development and growth for women, but there was a new era at the university. The previous administration had women in top leadership positions throughout the university. There was a history of sponsoring women faculty to participate in programs such as HERS (Higher Education Resource Services) Leadership Institute, ACE (American Council on Education) fellowships, and institutes at other local universities. The new administration at this time espoused support of women leadership development and enrichment for faculty, but with limited resources during financial difficulties, it did not prioritize those promises.

The principles used to create and shape the LEAD model framework are ones that can work in multiple contexts – not only in higher education. It draws from

DOI: 10.4324/9781003057208-1

the collective expertise and experiences of its members and will not be the same from institution to institution. It hasn't been the same across the many years of this group at this one institution. Instead, when using a feminist group praxis methodology that allows for organic discussions, agenda creation, shared group leadership facilitation, and individuals expressing their ideas of leadership in their own ways, change and development occur.

This is not unique to our institution. Women faculty only hold 32% of full rank professors positions, yet there are more faculty that identify as women than men across the country (Colorado Women's College, 2013). Factors that impact women from moving into full rank and leadership positions include time, balance of home and work demands, as well as sociocultural barriers within institutions that prevent women's strengths from being recognized as key assets for leadership roles.

We were in a unique position where we knew that in order to enact change and support our own development, we needed to mentor ourselves and provide for leadership enrichment. That was many years ago. At that time, the three of us decided to support our own leadership development. As we met to discuss a development plan, we realized we were not alone in this need. If we felt the need for this support, then we knew others would as well. We were in faculty leadership roles and making individual decisions for our own careers to move forward and decided to invite others to join us on this journey. We knew that we weren't looking for a formal leadership development journey – workshops filled with skills that we needed to acquire where the focus was on "just add women and stir" (Minnich, 2005). We knew we needed development that built upon our strengths as women in academia from distinct fields. We were in the early stages of our leadership development and also needed a safe space to explore these topics to express vulnerabilities and apprehension about leadership roles. We wanted to include other voices besides our own as we self-mentored each other.

The members of this group come from the fields of psychology, sociology, sciences, the arts, and education. Leadership Enrichment and Development, LEAD, was born from this need and desire. The core group worked to strategically support the advancement of each other. Since the group's establishment in 2015, the membership has taken leadership positions within the faculty and administration of Lesley University, as well as leadership roles in professional organizations and communities, and others have retired or taken positions elsewhere.

Invitation to the Table

In order to have others join us in this exploration, we invited core faculty, those permanently contracted at our university, who self-identified as women, to join us for this organic process to see what would unfold. We found a time in our university schedule that was not booked with classes or other standing meetings (a nearly impossible task to this day). The invitation was for lunch and an exploration of individual leadership development. We had lots of questions from curious colleagues, "Was this for those already in an administrative role?" "Do I have to go into an administrative role to join?" It should be noted that the term leadership implies administration and association with a formal role in the university. We immediately knew this was a topic to explore – What does leadership from your position/role mean? As mentioned earlier, 14 of the original 19 members have gone to leadership roles within the university setting.

New members were joining the group and outlining their own continued leadership development plans for themselves. More importantly, there was more of a shared collective ownership of the mentoring and stewardship of others within the university setting. The LEAD framework highlights that women's leadership development is not just about the individual women that are developed and ultimately promoted; it is about shifting the perception of an institution and the way in which space is made at the table to have shared power in a deliberate way. We are not saying that everyone in the group and at the university has felt the same shift and change, but through the LEAD model, we have seen subtle changes. It also highlights the need for responsive leadership development models that do not simply *add women and stir* (Minnich, 2005). This will be highlighted in more detail in Chapter 4 as models of leadership development will be compared.

We entered this space as individuals not only with different career experiences and perspectives, but with different expectations as well. Some members came expecting skill-based workshops that would teach us how to be a leader – which is a common development model (Storberg-Walker & Natt och Dag, 2018). Some members came wanting to connect with other colleagues to talk about challenges they were experiencing in their roles and positions, while other members came with an intent to change the landscape of leadership and the perception of leadership at our institution (van Esch et al., 2017). This became a key learning goal of the group – how can institutional change occur? Some members had a history of being in leadership positions during the previous administration and wanted to take part in an initiative to support a new generation of self-identified women leaders at the university. We had to make a space in our group for all members to not only get what they needed but more importantly grow and learn from each other.

What Is Feminist Leadership in LEAD?

Professional, personal, aspirational, problem-solving and negotiation, making power visible, naming it, replacing it, strategically building it, formal leadership, informal leadership, relational leadership, nurturing relationships, creating culture change in small and large ways, and influencing. The facilitators of the group worked to unpack what it meant to have a feminist approach (Belenky et al., 1997; Jordan, 2017; Crabtree & Sapp, 2003; Minnich, 2005) to this group – we sought not to default to a "do this to be a leader" or embark on a hierarchical skill-based/competency-based approach. We aimed to create a space that centered women's experiences while intentionally decentering power differentials among our group membership. By co-constructing agendas and working collaboratively, together we created LEADers.

Guided by principles of feminist group process and pedagogy (Belenky et al., 1997; Jordan, 2017; Crabtree & Sapp, 2003, Minnich, 2005), the members of the group co-constructed the LEAD methodology. Focusing on a variety of developmental tasks and topics, explorations of literature as catalysts for examination of individual lived experiences, and engaged discussions, participants explored the realities of leading as women in higher education today. Using a feminist praxis (Maher & Tetrault, 2001) in application to leadership development utilizes individual members' perspectives to form and shape the experience that is co-created. At the foundation of it is that women co-construct knowledge together through shared experiences and conversation (Belenky et al., 1997). The facilitators resisted creating detailed agendas but instead crafted activities and probes where we could first get to know each other and build trust and more importantly confidentiality. We will outline the methods we used later in this chapter and subsequent chapters in more detail.

We should be clear that the LEAD methods, which will be highlighted throughout the book, are not to be simply replicated for the same impact on individuals and institutions. Rather, the LEAD framework is suggested as a set of guiding principles and practices for others to consider as leadership development experiences are created in other settings.

Our LEAD Participants: Who Came to the Table?

The women that originally came to the table came from different disciplines and perspectives. The three original facilitators had planned to invite women leaders. It is important to note that our original call was for self-identified women faculty. The distinction of core (long-term contract) faculty and administration was an important factor at this time. The university was in a state of great debate over university governance and financial decisions, which prompted the adjunct and core faculties to move to unionize. When LEAD started, unionization efforts were underway. All this added to the complexity of the roles individuals were playing within their places in the university, leaving some feeling more safe than others. The group's premise relied on safety and confidentiality. Due to our commitment to creating a safe place, the repeated refrain was and still is even seven years later: Who is included? Who is not? Little did we predict that a leadership development group that espouses supporting women leadership development would have to grapple with this tenuous question: What happens when a member moves into a formal leadership role? Are they allowed to continue? When we started LEAD, it was our response to a specific need, a gap in our knowledge, and a desire to do it right. Because financial resources were not available, we resorted to a Do-It-Ourselves leadership development approach. What the facilitators knew was that we sought to create a place/process for convening women interested in exploring leadership development, and that we would do so in a collective way by creating space, joining together as a group through the co-creation of group norms, and readings to share and interrogate. We determined the need for confidentiality of shared topics, clarity of and respect for boundaries, especially critical as a group of women operating in the same professional home. As the structure of the group evolved and membership became more consistent and stable, the group evolved to provide relational support through a dialogic structure, creating the opportunity for meaningful discussion about our lived experiences as women faculty, and the realities of our work, the daily challenges, obstacles, successes, and opportunities. We became a community that supported each other through dilemmas of practice while celebrating each other's and our collective successes. Our space welcomed the multiple identities held by our members: parent, grandparent, caregiver, sandwich generation, partners, and the joys and sorrows that those roles carry and bring into the workspace. LEAD fostered the identification of individual and collective aspirations of our members, honoring the places our members hoped to travel professionally and personally.

Setting the Table

The provost at the time worked with the directors of The Women's Center at the university to set budget priorities. Through this relationship, LEAD was put on the table as a priority to support women faculty leadership development. A modest budget was earmarked for this work; it provided for meals, books, and "takeaways" from each meeting. Although it was not the amount of money allocated to women's leadership development in the previous administration, it was appreciated, especially during a period of enrollment challenges at the university that caused tighter financial constraints to be placed on programs, thus making fewer resources available. At the time we began LEAD, none of us were senior leaders, though a couple of our members had been in past stages of their careers. While some sought leadership roles, others did not; but all of us were highly experienced faculty as well as local or middle managers able to influence change in our departments and programs. As such, and over time, after building trust, connection, and friendships, together we strategized to address challenges – relational and structural – individual and collective. Thus, the group became an exemplar of the feminist group process, collectively, through the sharing of and growing power and strength within the group, we were able to influence the developmental trajectories of our members. Looking back on this, the outcomes of this group and the advances achieved by our members may have a greater impact and staying power than if we had invested in participation in some external women's leadership development program.

The need for leadership development for women faculty at our institution reflects the national trends in higher education, with increasing numbers of women aspiring to and fulfilling senior leadership positions across all levels of academia (https://www.acenet.edu/Documents/Womens-Rep-in-Higher-Ed-Leadership-Around-the-World.pdf).

Over the last 25 years, numerous fields, including medicine, law, engineering, STEM, PreK-12 education, and business, have instituted leadership development programs specific to women in a concerted effort to increase opportunities and prepare women for leadership roles. Making gender visible, naming it, and strategically building responses: Gender and power are central problems of feminist theorizing, research, and practice. In LEAD, they are central to our focus, the way we approach our work together, and supporting each other's personal developmental goals. During group sessions, we center and make visible women's lived experiences, while naming and revealing the structural problems located within one's individual experiences. Struggling with balancing the demands of the faculty role while mothers, partners, and caregivers to aging parents, while personally deeply felt, become seen and understood through a social and cultural framework. Peer support for each other's personal challenges, when seen through an institutional lens, has provided the support and a sense of empowerment necessary to manage personal goals and aspirations within an institutional framework (Acker, 2006).

Lesley University, originally founded as a normal school in 1909, under the progressive leadership of Edith Lesley, forged a new movement in kindergarten education, setting in motion new educational and professional pathways for women in the fields of education and the helping professions. Over time, Lesley University changed, became larger, and became more expansive in its educational offerings, all while preserving its central mission of educating women. In 2004, Lesley began admitting men to the undergraduate college, thus changing the composition of the university, and some might argue its direction. Many faculty and administrators remained committed to progressive education infused with a feminist ethos as the college changed with a new population of students and evolving leadership. During the next 15 years, the university was led by two male presidents and male provosts, and at the time LEAD started, senior leadership and school deans were dominated by men. How this compositional makeup influenced the culture of the university is beyond the scope of this discussion, yet what was particularly obvious, when we started LEAD, is that the organizational leadership was male-dominated and provided little explicit mentoring and leadership development opportunities for women faculty. Underneath the senior leadership, women faculty dominated faculty ranks, and despite the numbers of women at the institution, the leadership style was task-oriented and transactional.

Though our experience at Lesley may feel particular to our own institutional day-to-day experiences, in fact, it is consistent with trends at other colleges and universities in the United States. Since the 1960's passage of the Civil Rights Act, doors previously closed to women's participation have been opened, including institutions of higher learning. Over the next 50+ years, the demographic of college student enrollment changed with female students outnumbering their male peers closing the gaps in fields of study previously dominated by men (Colorado Women's College, 2013). This shifting demographic reality cuts across institutional types and fields of study. In tandem, the numbers of women holding faculty positions increased, in some areas more rapidly than others. The last 50 years has resulted in a substantial cultural shift, with women dominating or nearly dominating every level of educational experience from high school through postgraduate programs and university faculty ranks. A major exception, however, persists in the area of university senior leadership, including academic deans and cabinet-level. To support the professional development of female faculty, colleges and universities offered specific leadership development programs within fields such as medicine, engineering, and business, and created mentorship and sponsorship pathways for faculty. Many well-known programs were developed by external organizations, providing space and time for women to leave campus to focus on developing and harnessing the skills required for top leadership roles, such as chairs, deans, and senior leadership. Organizations including HERS (https://www.hersnetwork.org) and ACE (https://www.acenet.edu) created environments for women to join cohorts to study, be supported, and practice skills and new ways of thinking, enabling a movement from the academic-scholar role to that of leader. Programs led by women for women created the space for women faculty to cultivate competence and confidence in order to navigate a hierarchical and patriarchal sociopolitical system.

Our LEADers

As indicated earlier, our group was self-selected. An invitation went out to all self-identified women core faculty, and those who were interested joined our initial meetings. The group included a blend of academic scholars and practitioners, scientists, and scholar practitioners. At that time, the original group did not contain any individuals who held a traditional administrative role – as defined by a job description. At the start of the group, our members ranged in age from the early 30s to the late 60s. Some had been at the university for less than five years, and others had been there for over 30 years. Of those veteran faculty members, several had been in what were considered traditional administrative leadership roles in the past but were not in an administrative role at the time the group formed. We spanned the ranks of faculty at our university, from instructor to assistant, associate to full professor.

We were also, and remain as of this writing, a relatively homogeneous group. Although our initial meetings did have more diversity in terms of racial and ethnic identities, that did not continue throughout the lifespan of the group. We have done a great deal of reflection on this issue and have been challenged by outside members on this issue. It is one that the group grapples with continually. Due to the fact that the group was and has remained self-selected, we have worked to make open invitations to all members of the faculty in a genuine way that does not assume the way to diversify is just to get "more diverse" members. We want to work to create a space where diversity is welcome, and individuals that would like support in their leadership development will find this group inclusive of the intersection of their identities as leaders in higher education. But the issue of who holds the power in the larger societal structures is present in our group as well – the real and perceived holding of the power. In many ways, the group evolved into an affinity group where individuals with similar identities explored a topic together.

What counts as leadership in the LEAD method? Formal Leadership, informal leadership, and relational leadership: We had no expectations, no bar to meet, and no goal to aspire to. While we never defined "leadership" in the initial design of LEAD, we soon came to understand that for our group, the definition of leadership happens in the formal, informal, and interstitial spaces of our lives. We welcomed women's unique/personal claims on how they lived in the world as leaders, including leadership in the private sphere of the family and homelife (Maternal Leadership), as leaders in the classroom/learning space (Teacher Leadership), and leaders in formal organizational settings including the university, political, and religious spaces. It is through this open/broad acceptance of the diverse ways we each lead that led us to the concept of self-leadership. Since our group developed, each member has had multiple roles and identities as a leader, some formal, others informal, and still others invisible. Yet, the LEAD group structure created a space where all our leadership identities were welcome, regardless of which ones were more salient or more in the background at a given moment in time. Our view of self-as-leaders, in our various contexts, were accepted and actively engaged in LEAD meetings. Our feminist group process provided the structure to support each other's forward movement as leaders, honoring each other's definitions and experiences of leadership.

A factor we had to consider was consistency of membership for relationship building and confidentiality as a key part of the group process. This meant that we asked members to prioritize a set time each month for participation in meetings, and after the second year, we closed membership in order to have time to build relationships. That helped members build trust and relationships with each other and truly created a confidential space for sharing, growing, and pushing back on each other about difficult topics. That was a benefit of the group and how it worked.

On the other hand, the perception of a closed group came back to challenge us in two ways. First, we appeared to be an exclusive, non-inclusive group with the closed nature of our membership in subsequent years. Second, we had to ask ourselves about the inclusion of women who moved into administrative roles as defined by the job description. Were we saying that once you had a formal leadership role, you were no longer welcome? What about members of the university community that were not on faculty contracts yet taught and were leading the institution in other ways? Should they be invited to join the table? As new faculty members joined the university community, the perceived exclusivity of the group grew in university conversations.

LEAD was initially met with excitement and eagerness from women faculty who sought participation. We had to deal with membership – who is in and who is not – not a particularly feminist way to start a feminist group.

The us versus them paradigm is not unusual. Research indicates that competition among women in leadership is prevalent and impacts women in their decision-making to choose formal leadership roles as well as advocating for leadership development support. One member of the group was faced with the question, "Why are you interested in leadership suddenly?" It was as if expanding scholarship and academic focus to leadership development and away from one's original line of scholarship in a field of study was not allowed or was a betrayal of others. Mavin (2006, 2008) and Mavin et al. (2018) highlight that women in leadership positions do so within the context of masculine competition and are therefore viewed as betraying others by taking on leadership positions. This has long been written about with Freire (2018) calling out "horizontal violence" as a perpetuation of male leadership norms and maintaining the disparity of genders in leadership positions. Would participating in such a group contribute to the problem of perceptions of "queen bees" and continue to reinforce gender hierarchies in the organization? How could such a group break up the female misogyny that was present at this time in the institution? The potential power of such would come from the recognition of the intersection of the different identities that each member had and how that perspective from those lived experiences could create leadership development as a group.

The question of how we are an intersectional feminist group was frequently reflected back to us. We had to recognize that while claiming to be open and collaborative, perhaps we were not. We had to frequently examine and check our assumptions about why some interested members of our community were not included, such as administrators who self-identify as women. Were we really open, collaborative, and engaging in true feminist practice when we are predominantly a group of white women faculty developing ourselves? Where is the promise of institutional change in this system and structure?

These questions did not go away. The question of belonging and who belongs is one that we are currently addressing by changing our working methods. We have worked to get information about the group and how it works for other members of the university community. We have made sure to reach out to all new faculty across the university. And we made the decision to open membership to all self-identifying women members of the university community – regardless of job title, position, or role in the university. It should be noted that these steps occurred just before March 2020, when the university, like many other institutions of higher education, went into a remote format for instructional and meetings with the COVID-19 pandemic. This obviously impacted our activities and progress at that time.

Opportunities for women's leadership development are popular and available. A Google search will result in a myriad of professional development opportunities, each interesting in their own way. Often, these are short experiences, taught or facilitated by leadership experts, arming completers with tools to take back to the workplace. The authors of this LEAD volume have participated in many over the years. In many ways, such opportunities feel like vitamin B12 shots, providing a vital dose of short-term skills to manage the complexities of the higher education environment. LEAD is different. Centering relationships, building new knowledge, skills, and ways of seeing self, through co-constructed processes, results in identity development/perhaps transformation, that moves us, as individual women leaders, and propels our individual and collective ability to create change and lasting impact on our professional communities.

LEAD Framework

The fundamental design of LEAD builds upon the important scholarship of relational cultural theorists, feminist epistemology, feminist group processes, and women's identity development. Locating these frameworks against the backdrop of higher education and institutional power made the LEAD group necessary and vital for the members, contributing to the longevity of the group's structure and process. In our first extended retreat, the group created our mission statement:

> *LEAD's mission is to engage women faculty in collaborative leadership that guides constructive dialogue so that groups are learning with and from one another as we move toward a common vision with a sense of contentment and accomplishment that nurtures and nourishes each of us.*

To examine the method by which we approached LEAD, we can identify the individual components of this guiding principle and describe their roles.

Engage

We were not interested in offering a series of workshops led by "experts" brought in to teach the rest of us about leadership. Not only would this have run counter to our feminist relational model, but we wanted to co-create something new with participants rather than simply deliver information to them.

The logistics of co-creating an agenda and sharing group facilitation, however, initially felt counterproductive to some of us who had greater familiarity (and, consequently, greater comfort) with traditional approaches and modes. Standard components of "effective" meeting management (e.g., agendas and supporting materials sent ahead of time, some variation of Robert's Rules of Order) and work-based training sessions (e.g., a list of objectives, an overview of materials to be presented), however, all privilege the leader in setting the priorities and direction of the group. Furthermore, the implicit assumption is that the leader has some degree of authority, information, or expertise that is greater than that of the group members.

The LEAD framework was built on an awareness of power, and we wanted power to be shared. Agendas are facilitated by the original members but then shaped and agreed upon by the members of the group. They usually come from sharing challenges and struggles or things recently experienced/learned in our professional lives. Example topics for agendas in the first year included talking about challenges we faced as women identified faculty including our own leadership development journeys, roles we had at other institutions or employers, striking the balance of life and work. We culminated our year with a day-long retreat where we re-visited our original intentions for the group and co-constructed a visual model of what LEAD was.

Fostering group members' engagement and not just attention and interest entailed disrupting the approach sanctioned by conventional wisdom (aka patriarchy) and shifting our measures of the success of the group to be more clearly focused on developing a relational process rather than output and "efficiency." LEAD holds that the key to engagement is the process that ensues and the discomfort that might come from not knowing the end result – from not meeting pre-determined learning objectives.

Women

There is an ongoing – and sometimes uncomfortable – public discourse about the reality that some groups that attempt homogeneity of membership (e.g., male-only country clubs and, prior to 2017, Boy Scouts of America) are labeled as non-inclusive and may, at times, be forced to accept a more diverse population. The argument becomes a "what about"-istic approach that challenges affinity groups or other groups that are created by and for specific, targeted membership should also be fully inclusive.

While the logic holds up from one angle, there is a key difference. Not unlike uninformed comments about the nonexistence of "White History Month" or a straight analog to Pride Month, the assertion that membership in an affinity group is discriminatory disregards the historical and contemporary impact of institutional biases, prejudice, discrimination (Woo, 2018), and – in this case – a patriarchal system that have played key roles in perpetuating the inequity. Ultimately, we decided that explicitly limiting group membership only to those who identified as women was going to be essential to the process.

Faculty

Criteria for inclusion in the group quickly morphed into criteria for exclusion, with the main "keep out" category being that of women faculty who were also in administrative positions. Of course, some degree of tension between faculty and administration is not uncommon in higher education. The genesis of the group coincided with a particularly intense period of contention and distrust between faculty and administration that, ultimately, resulted in core faculty unionization.

With a lack of foresight – or perhaps confidence – in how LEAD would affect our personal trajectories, we did not leave room to re-examine the criteria as many LEAD members moved into faculty leadership and administrative positions. This created not only hard feelings with some supportive and interested women administrators but also multiple awkward conversations in which we re-justified to one another why someone could remain in LEAD despite a change in professional status while someone with a similar status could not join.

By 2019, it was clear that the original criteria that were set in a substantively different culture were inappropriate and counterproductive. With an unavoidable awareness of the ways the leadership development needs of self-identified women staff and administrators remained unmet, LEAD invited all self-identified women at Lesley – regardless of rank or position – to join. Due to the timing of this decision falling immediately before the onset of the COVID-19 pandemic, we have been unable to revisit the expanded role of LEAD at Lesley.

Collaborative Leadership

Different from a touchy-feely group in which everyone needed to agree (because in a group of "nice" women, how was there going to be disagreement at the Norming stage of group development?), it was clear that we had both capital L leaders and lower-case l leaders. We also had academics who felt it was their responsibility to be the voice of expertise and experience, sometimes to the detriment of others exploring their own leadership understandings. This made group dynamics in a collaborative setting more challenging – a lesson we all needed to learn from to enact change at the institution. Early on, there were some direct challenges to the leadership, with a suggestion that the co-founders were not the appropriate people for the task, accompanied by an implication that budget decisions should be made by all group members. Finding the balance between co-construction and consensus while adhering to the tenets of our feminist relational model was, at times, challenging to those of us more accustomed to a traditional group leadership hierarchy. For instance, one member of the group shared her frustration with news she received from the promotion committee and the group met to problem solve how she could use the outlined process to deal with the negative response and address it accordingly. Another member was facing a hostile situation in the larger faculty audience in public meetings and the group problem solved how to proactively engage in the conversation publicly and dispel rumors and false statements being made against that member. Again, because we maintained confidentiality as a group and demonstrated that in our actions, people grew in their comfort and trust in the group to bring very difficult and challenging situations to the group for collective input, problem solving, and support.

Constructive Dialogue

It was tempting to use our time as a gripe session to complain about university life. That would have kept us hyper-focused on the problems we were facing or the shared experiences of inequity we were dealing with at any given point in time. A more generous description of this would be to say we debated how much of a support group we wanted to be.

One could argue that there is certainly value in the supportive aspect of a group, as Yalom (2020) identified the universality and instillation of hope as a curative factor in group therapy models. For this group to be transformative, however, we needed to do more than just feel good and feel supported when we left the meeting. Additionally, we did not need to have a series of monologues determined by who was dealing with the biggest issues in any given meeting. Even when we were facing personal or specific issues, the group took a strategic approach that weaved in bigger-picture, structural components of the institution. Over time, we worked on strategies to facilitate this dynamic including time limits on individual speaking contributions, focused check-in questions, and small groups to address particular issues.

Groups

Whether it is the trope of women going to the restroom *en masse* or the more sobering reason women may accompany one another to a dark parking lot, the idea of there being safety in numbers is undeniable. Even setting aside more of Yalom's curative factors of groups and turning instead to Maslow's need for belonging, there are multiple benefits to a group model. Aligned with the feminist relational model, utilizing the power of a group further removed us from the temptation of a mentor/mentee dynamic in which one individual or identified cluster of individuals were deemed to be the "experts" who would impart their knowledge to the others. As individual members within a group, we were self-mentoring each other; hence, strength comes from the collective of the group.

Learning With and From One Another

Together, we explored a number of shared texts,[1] articles, and media TED Talks paired with facilitated discussion. Selections originally came from the facilitators but eventually came from suggestions of the group. As stated previously, the group membership spanned a range of academic ranks, professional roles, years of experience, fields of study, depth of feminist or gender studies knowledge, and length of tenure at Lesley. We learned from one another about actual funds of knowledge (e.g., feminist theory), processes internal to our institution (e.g., Rank and Promotion) and the frameworks used by different disciplines to explain shared experiences. We often reflected on shared experiences through our respective lenses. For instance, teacher educators with expertise in literacy lead us in guided reading and discussion of particular texts. Members would bring in selected passages or quotes to share for reflection and discussion. Another member acted as a facilitator to engage the group in an exercise to envision LEAD through a visual medium. Additionally, as we grew in our trust and saw the enactment of the confidentiality norm, we used the space more for mutual problem solving around difficult situations, career advancement, and collective problem solving around larger issues members found themselves in at the university.

Common Vision

By 2016, the group was coordinating internal grant applications to be as strategic as possible in moving a women's leadership agenda forward. The individual projects and interests had coalesced into something larger that included all. We would strategize internal grants for funding of retreats, meals provided, and books for all to receive.

Contentment

The establishment of group norms (Aronson & Mills, 1959) to guide our interactions and explicitly revisit shared expectations puts each of us in a position of responsibility to not harbor unspoken resentment or dissatisfaction with some aspect of LEAD or a LEAD meeting. Again, a feminist relational approach with somewhat flattened delineations of power creates a structure that supports expressions of disagreement. Checking in about our collective norms became a ritual we use to this day:

- Appreciate confidentiality, honesty, and safety.
- Be direct and don't sugarcoat.
- Explore dimensions of leadership.
- Don't put limitations on the expression of leadership for each other.
- Understand the fluidity of the group across meetings.

- It's okay to say "No."
- Do not reject what we consider to be male (leadership qualities or approaches).

The unspoken expectation was that contentment would come, not from everything working out "right" or going our way, but from the confidence in knowing there was a space and culture to be fully seen, heard, known, and acknowledged. An important part of working in a feminist space is to set norms for how we will work together. Norm-setting and affirming are elements taken from other feminist working groups and were key parts of all our meetings (Eberhardt, 1994; Bolen, 1999). Norms must be generated by the group using them. At the beginning of each meeting, therefore, the norms were revisited with an openness to revisions. Some of the consistent norms included confidentiality and allowing for multiple definitions of "leadership." We use the norms to start the meeting and reflect on what is working well and how we could alter our work together for a future meeting. It should be noted that members of the group have taken the group norm process to other meetings and circles in the university as a lesson learned from the LEAD framework. Most recently, a school within the university used the process to create norms to help engage in the work of examining anti-racist teacher education and practices as a group.

Accomplishment

As noted previously, most of the original group members have ascended within the formal ranks of academia. Ironically, these accomplishments reduced the amount of time, energy, and mental bandwidth we had to convene or coordinate LEAD meetings. We often joke that "we are too busy leading to hold a LEAD meeting for our own development." As part of celebrating each other's accomplishments, we encourage each other to share news and recent "wins" as part of our group time. We also prod each other to not minimize or reframe an accomplishment or challenge met, as women often do to take up less space. There are not many spaces in the university environment where one can find refuge, care, and solidarity. A primary focus of LEAD, regardless of the agenda topic, was to build in nurturance and an ethic of care (Noddings, 2013) into our practices.

Nurtures and Nourishes

There is a fair amount of overlap between the concepts of nurture and nourish, as they are both, ultimately, synonyms for caring for and fostering growth of someone or something. In fact, we probably could have used "cultivate" and covered it all. The differentiation may be (though, to be honest, we probably didn't put much intentional consideration into it) that nurturing more broadly encompasses creating an overall environment that encourages development, while nourishing is more specific to the concept of the provision of the elements necessary for sustenance.

In clinical practice (Barker, 2010), it's not unusual for women clients to describe themselves as being "selfish" when they just state their needs, even with little expectation that those needs can or should be met. It was important to create a new environment that shifted these expectations in ways that extended past the LEAD meetings themselves. We wanted the women to feel held, seen, and valued.

It was tempting (and would have been more cost-effective) to offer LEAD meetings as a "Lunch and Learn" series in which attendees were responsible for bringing their own lunch. The next most cost-effective approach would have been to order sandwiches or pizza. We are fed in any number of ways, however.

We opted, therefore, to provide carefully selected and beautifully presented meals at each meeting. This ensured that everyone who attended had "real food" to eat as opposed to something they grabbed on their way out the door – if they had time. It also allowed us to have a shared, communal meal, further developing a sense of cohesiveness (Yalom, 2020).

We also always offer a tangible object that has some element of beauty or whimsy for each member to keep. Easily dismissed as a trinket, these objects – sometimes symbolic, sometimes practical – serve as a concrete reminder of the connection and support of the group. Akin to a talisman, if not a transitional object, the physical takeaway becomes imbued with the positive association to their experience in LEAD and receiving them became a valued and signature moment of our group.

LEAD's Impact on Leadership Identity

Our invitation to LEAD opened the opportunity for women interested in exploring women's leadership development to join together and, through a shared and co-constructed agenda, give and receive that which was personally meaningful. Perhaps one of the powerful elements of our method, as with other feminist groups that exist with a consistent membership and meeting schedule, is that something new, and greater than the individual members is created and cultivated. The feminist process in the community generated new ideas and ways of seeing and responding, resulting in confidence and competence for creating change and new ways of understanding. When we began LEAD, we did not have a vision of where we would travel as a group. The power of the group led us in important directions for the individual members and collectively as a group of women leaders. If we consider formal leadership, members of our group moved in and out and into leadership roles (two deans of faculty, two chairs of Faculty Assembly, program directors, department chairs, senior leaders in our union). Our feminist pedagogy of dialogue, relational mentorship, and strategic problem-solving supported our members to bring to voice personal and professional aspirations and to work through the barriers to leaning in and stepping up. For others in LEAD, it was serving as wise counsel to other members, and still for others, it was talking through political challenges, and conflict, including the experiences of bullying and policing. Developing courage to manage and address (often through collaboration and a team approach) harmful institutional practices or negligence became important elements of our regular meeting agendas. Unfortunately, while problems did not always resolve, members developed strategy, power, and strength to take on challenges. Our feminist group process was and is the central vehicle for harnessing powerful personal and professional outcomes for members of LEAD.

This feminist praxis – the intersection of the experiential and theoretical, interrogated through the lenses of gender and power – became a central organizing principle of the group and an intentional design of our LEAD approach. We could have chosen other methods or models for our group and could have decided to be fully inclusive of all genders in the design and structure of the group. In fact, many of our male faculty peers could argue they also share similar work-life balance problems and navigate the complexities of balancing family and caregiving demands with work. However, we assert that the patriarchal structure of higher education, including our own institution, even our own, formerly a women's college, necessitated that we create a space exclusively for women faculty, a space where gender sat at the center and was a shared and dominant lens through which our concerns, needs, and opportunities for growth would be addressed. However, our group membership, while all women identified, differed in other ways, including age, religion, social class, sexuality, and differences in professional status. It is also important to acknowledge that power is and never was completely equal, yet during our regular meetings we worked hard to share the space, working diligently to make all voices heard even when that was challenging, the result of a highly successful group of professional women. A major challenge for our group is that we were all largely a group of white heterosexual cis-gendered women, thus, a group overflowing in status, power, and privilege. The lack of racial diversity has been and continues to be a problem for the membership of our group. This structural reality limits what is possible to create and accomplish within this group. We continue to work to remedy this challenge by opening up LEAD to a broader range of participants from our university, thus seeking to create greater diversity among our members. As we wrestle with this important challenge, our feminist approach to the group, through the sharing of facilitation and the co-construction of meeting agendas, was and is an intentional act to manage power differences as much as possible.

As highlighted earlier in this chapter, it has also put a spotlight on the inequities of leadership development and access to resources within an institution based on other intersections of identities: race, ethnicity, and gender expression. A LEAD model is based on the assumption that recognition of the intersections of identities is key to leadership development, and self-mentoring models must harness the power of those identities and the complexities that come from them. In subsequent chapters of this book, particular LEAD group methods will be discussed in more detail with a connection to a particular understanding that occurred for the group. We offer these not as a recipe to just add to other similar model groups but as examples of how the members of the group used tools from their own various disciplines to bring back to the group opportunities for growth and learning together. We do not suggest readers just follow this book like a how-to manual, but rather problem solve your own ways of looking at members' identities, leadership roles, and professional development goals to co-construct a group agenda that pulls from the strengths that come from these complexities.

LEADing You to Our Table

The chapters in this volume share our stories and the topics we believe are important for women aspiring to, or in leadership roles. A brief synopsis of each chapter is located later. A *Kitchen Table* epilogue closes our conversations with you, the reader, as a final chapter.

This first chapter, *Invitation to LEAD*, describes the context and formation of LEAD. The LEAD framework and approach were shared, setting the context for the rest of the chapters that follow.

Chapter 2 describes the analysis of the oral narratives of women faculty in higher education. The narratives were initially shared during a fall 2016 retreat and then later in interviews during the summer of 2020. Key moments in the individual journeys of women on their pathway to leadership are shared.

Chapter 3 analyzes barriers to women's entrance into higher education leadership positions and to their movement through the leadership hierarchy beyond mid-level positions. The analysis draws on postmodern feminist and critical race theory perspectives. The many variables that shape the low number of women in senior leadership positions in higher education are discussed.

Chapter 4 initially examines the most cited formal leadership theories in the literature. Then, contemporary leadership development practices in line with feminist relational perspective development are shared. The chapter also identifies distinctive competencies deemed to be important for current leaders with a lens toward the development of women in higher education.

Chapter 5 presents the current literature of women leadership development programs in the fields of PreK-12 public education, higher education, business, and engineering/STEM. Potential barriers to the development of women's leadership are investigated. The chapter highlights effective practices to advance women leaders and shares the results of a survey conducted of 140 women in leadership positions.

Chapter 6 explores the importance of mentoring women faculty in higher education. Five types of developmental relationships for women as they move into higher leadership positions are described: mentors, sponsors, peers, executive coaches, and learning partners. These types of relationships are further illustrated by the lived experiences of several women faculty members at one university.

Chapter 7 describes the Girlhood Project, a relational learning community of middle and high school girls and university students mentored by Emerging Girlhood Scholars, doctoral students, and the founding director, one of the editors/authors of this volume. The community was guided by feminist group processes and a belief in the power of relationships to foster the development of voice, self-knowledge, identity, and competencies of confidence and self-authorship. This chapter focuses on the development of voice and leader identity among the university students who facilitated The Girlhood Project. TGP and LEAD share a number of pedagogical similarities, underscoring the importance of relational learning and leading at any stage of the professional developmental journey.

Chapter 8 delineates one expansion of the LEAD model and discusses how peer mentoring groups can support women as they navigate their leadership path. Drawing on the experiences of a LEAD Mastermind group, insights into the inherent value of promoting gender equity, enriching women's leadership journeys, and creating inclusive environments that leverage the strength of women in leadership roles are shared.

Lastly, we share a brief epilogue in Chapter 9. Almost a decade after LEAD's inception, the authors and editors of *Invitation to LEAD* gathered via Zoom for a Kitchen Table conversation. Guided by several questions outlined in this chapter, the group reflected on our leadership identities and the ways our involvement with LEAD affected our journeys as individuals and as a collective.

Note

1 Brown, B. (2018). *Dare to lead: Brave work. Tough conversations. Whole hearts*. Random House.
DeWelde, K., & Stepnick, A. (Eds.). (2014). *Disrupting the culture of silence*. Routledge.
Hill, A. (2012). *Reimagining equality: Stories of gender, race and finding home*. Beacon Press.
Longman, K., & Madsen, S. (Eds.). (2014). *Women & leadership in higher education*. Information Age.
Madsen, S. (Ed.). (2018). *Handbook of research on gender and leadership* (Research Handbooks in Business and Management series). Edward Elgar.

References

Acker, J. (2006). Inequality regimes: Gender, class, and race in organizations. *Gender and Society*, *20*(4), 441–464. http://www.jstor.org/stable/27640904

Aronson, E., & Mills, J. (1959). The effect of severity of initiation on liking for a group. *The Journal of Abnormal and Social Psychology*, *59*(2), 177–181. https://doi.org/10.1037/h0047195

Barker, M. (2010). Self-care and relationship conflict. *Sexual & Relationship Therapy*, *25*(1), 37–47. https://doi.org/10.1080/14681990903479904

Belenky, M., Clinchy, B., & Goldberger, N. (1997). *Women's ways of knowing: The development of self, voice, and mind* (Tenth anniversary edition). Basic Books.

Bolen, J. S. (1999). *The millionth circle: How to change ourselves and the world.* Conari Press.

Colorado Women's College. (2013). *Benchmarking women's leadership in the United States*. Colorado Women's College, University of Denver.

Crabtree, R. D., & Sapp, D. A. (2003). Theoretical, political, and pedagogical challenges in the feminist classroom: Our struggles to walk the walk. *College Teaching, 51*(4), 131–140. https://doi.org/10.1080/87567550309596428

Eberhardt, L. Y. (1994). *Working with women's groups*. Whole Person Associates.

Freire, P. (2018). *Pedagogy of the oppressed* (4th ed.). Bloomsbury Academic.

https://www.acenet.edu/Documents/Womens-Rep-in-Higher-Ed-Leadership-Around-the-World.pdf

Jordan, J. V. (2017). Relational-cultural theory: The power of connection to transform our lives. *Journal of Humanistic Counseling, 56*(3), 228–243. https://doi.org/10.1002/johc.12055

Lennon, T. (2012). *Benchmarking women's leadership in the United States*. University of Denver.

Maher, F. A., & Tetrault, M. K. T. (2001). *The feminist classroom: Dynamics of gender, race, and privilege*. Rowman & Littlefield Publishers.

Mavin, S. (2006). Venus envy: Problematizing solidarity behavior and queen bees. *Women in Management Review, 21*(4), 264–276.

Mavin, S. (2008). Queen bees, wannabees and afraid to bees: No more best enemies for women in management. *British Journal of Management, 19*(1), 75–84.

Mavin, S., Grandy, G., & Williams, J (2018). Theorizing women leaders' negative relations with other women. In S. Madsen (Ed.), *Handbook of research on gender and leadership*. Elgar.

Minnich, E. K. (2005). *Transforming knowledge* (2nd ed.). Temple University Press.

Noddings, N. (2013). *Caring: A relational approach to ethics and moral education* (2nd ed.). University of California Press.

Pasque, P., & Simpson, E. (2013). Women's status in higher education: Equity matters by Elizabeth J. Allan (review). *The Review of Higher Education, 36*(3), 426–427. https://doi.org/10.1353/rhe.2013.0032

Storberg-Walker, J., & Natt och Dag, K. (2018) Creativity in theorizing for women and leadership: A multi-paradigm perspective. In S. Madsen (Ed.), *Handbook on research on gender and leadership*. Elger.

van Esch, C., Assylkham, K., & Bilimoria, D. (2017). Using organization and management science theories to understand women and leadership. In S. Madsen (Ed.), *Handbook on research on gender and leadership*. Elger.

Woo, B. (2018). Racial discrimination and mental health in the USA: Testing the reverse racism hypothesis. *Journal of Racial and Ethnic Health Disparities, 5*(4), 766–773.

Yalom, I. D. (2020). *The theory and practice of group psychotherapy* (6th ed.). Basic Books.

2 Mapping the Leadership Heart

Barbara Steckel

As described in Chapter 1, a key part of the LEAD framework are interactive experiences that are often member-led, immersive, reflective experiences coming from the discipline of members. Using the co-constructed norms of the group members, dig deeper into their own development in a safe, supportive environment. In this chapter, I write about one of the experiences held during a retreat in the fall of 2016 where we collaborated on the exploration of our leadership journeys and identity development over our careers to collaborate on a book proposal. Where this took us was vastly different than many of us expected – another key element of the LEAD framework – where the process was more important than the learning objectives.

As we planned for this retreat, I was asked to call upon my expertise in language and literacy development to craft an icebreaker. I called the exercise *Mapping the Leadership Heart* because it involved creating an artistically rendered, heart-shaped outline of personal and professional experiences to be shared. What was intended to be a simple icebreaker serendipitously became a pivotal moment that led us to a trove of rich data to draw from as we considered the content of the forthcoming book. The data were embedded in the shared personal narratives that described the complex, multifaceted journey of each woman's leadership development. I will begin by describing this common experience we had and how it set the stage for a deeper relational understanding of the group. I will capture that moment in time of our leadership identity journeys and what we learned from it to use in our further development of LEAD.

The second part of the chapter extends beyond the description of the original retreat activity to include data gleaned from a set of follow-up interviews that took place four years later, during the summer of 2020. The follow-up interviews were conducted with five of the original attendees who volunteered and were willing to do the work of delving into shared self-reflection and analysis to gain further insight into their personal evolution as feminist leaders.

I present a portrait of each of the five participants to illuminate their reflections on leadership development. The chapter culminates with my analysis of emerging themes regarding women in leadership roles and how these themes

DOI: 10.4324/9781003057208-2

may depart from many of the traditional paradigms of leadership within many male-dominated organizational structures and demonstrated within the research literature on the topic of feminist leadership development (O'Brien et al., 2023).

My Leadership Journey

My own leadership journey is distributed within K-12 and higher education. It may be worth noting that I grew up in the Bronx, New York, and I am the first

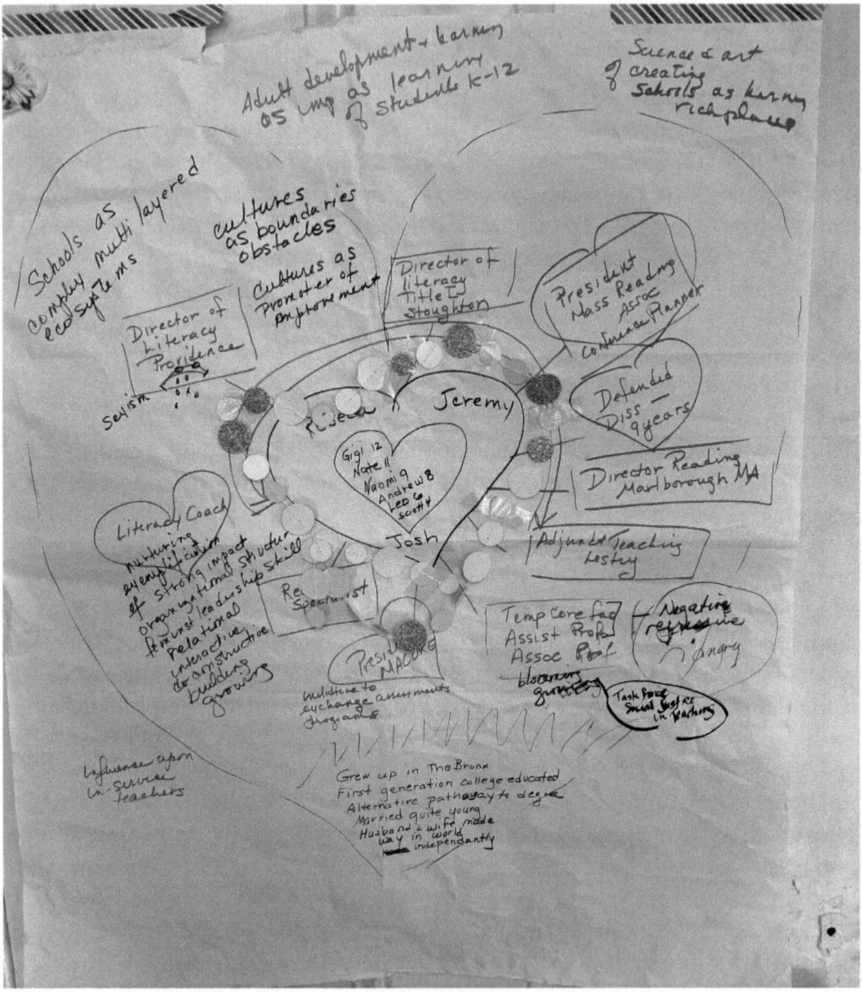

Figure 2.1 The author's leadership heart showing her journey from her youth in the Bronx to her expanding leadership roles across her career.

university-educated member of my family. I began my career as a substitute teacher, a classroom teacher, and a reading specialist. I took a risk when I moved into the position of literacy coach in Boston at the time when coaching was in its pioneer days. It was a rather new and radical idea in public education to have teachers coach other teachers to improve outcomes for students. I was a successful coach due to my focus on relationship building and reciprocal sharing of knowledge, valuing what colleagues brought to the table. I became president of my state's professional literacy organization, simultaneously moving on to administrative Director of Literacy in a school district. Academia became my second career after I completed my Doctorate in Education. Currently I am a Professor and Reading Specialist Program Director with a school of education in Cambridge, Massachusetts. Although I have previously experienced leadership within the field of literacy and public education from many perspectives, my current LEAD colleagues have meant a great deal to me as far as my own development as a leader within the newer context of the university setting.

For those who know me, it would be no surprise that the narrative sharing activity that I volunteered to facilitate at the original retreat was steeped in literacy and language-related activities. The activities included time for reflecting, thinking, and evoking memories, pre-organizing ideas about important moments, composing and sharing personal oral narratives, listening to the shared narratives of others, making personal connections, and expressing shared empathy. Let me tell you a bit more about this activity and how it influenced our group.

The Retreat

A tool in the LEAD framework is making space for each other and prioritizing the time with members for the work. During each year of LEAD, we held annual retreats, half-day and full-day, to focus together on our individual and collective development. As we planned to explore our leadership development and potential book, we knew that we needed more time together and time away from day-to-day life in order to focus and build relationships. Why not get away?

Ten of us came together on a rather brisk and picturesque fall weekend in October 2016. The women in our group had put a temporary hold on life and obligations for that weekend to make it possible to gather in an old ship captain's home in a New England fishing town that was reserved as the site for the retreat. The time spent together was dramatic, punctuated with the outside wind pounding shutters against window frames and surging waters rising against the adjacent wharf. We were filled with anticipation regarding who the new president of this country would be, and the air was electric with possibilities for our nation as well as future personal and professional possibilities for each of us. The purpose of the retreat was to outline a book proposal that would illuminate the process of leadership development for women faculty in higher education. In order to draft a viable proposal, we wanted to capture several themes related to leadership development from a feminist stance that were embedded in the lived experiences of the women in our group.

Mapping the Leadership Heart

Mapping the Heart (Heard, 1999) is a pre-writing organizing activity for young writers, inspiring recall, reflection, and critical analysis of the influential people, places, and events in one's life. Being a teacher at heart (no pun intended), it occurred to me that this powerful technique for young writers would be an evocative exercise for a mature audience as well. The activity prompts writers to recall and record words and images, people, places, and symbols that are meaningful elements in their lives. The images are strategically arranged, sized possibly according to relative importance, and categorized as part of the process of surfacing and sorting the most meaningful or influential aspects of one's lived experiences.

Why not apply this wonderful, creative, artistic experience to LEAD group members? We were planning to gather together to draft a proposal for a book regarding academic women and leadership, therefore a pre-writing organizer would be just the thing to begin our writing process. The exercise of Mapping the Heart would help each woman to recall the narrative of their developmental journey toward leadership and reflect their leadership identity development. It would help each of us to use the gift of time during the weekend retreat to relive the formative experiences, obstacles, and encouragements that shaped their leadership development.

The exercise served to evoke unexpectedly rich oral narratives that we shared with each other during the weekend retreat. The activity had multiple positive outcomes. What was intended as a pre-writing organizer and icebreaker serendipitously became a framing activity requiring deep self-reflection and sharing – again relying on the norms that we co-constructed as a group particularly Give Space and Make Space and of course confidentiality. We used chart paper and craft supplies to organize our reflections and create the hearts independently in different locations around the inn. Then we shared our oral narratives with the rest of the group. The process felt intimate to us. It led members of our group on a new pathway toward strengthening understanding of self, developing empathy for each other, and as a result, solidifying our cohesiveness as a group of women with shared interest. The narratives included difficult personal and professional challenges common to many women to which we could easily relate. The act of sharing our lived experiences in this intimate setting helped us to surface the themes that would shape our book proposal.

The themes we hoped to explore were to define leadership generally and capture the ways in which leadership is often manifested by women in particular. We wanted to deepen our understanding of the personal barriers as well as the cultural and societal barriers that marginalize women and other minorities. It was our hope that these deepening understandings would be enriching to each of us as individuals, strengthen our group process, and be reflected in the book we would produce. Furthermore, we wanted to share insights regarding obstacles and opportunities for leadership as we support one another within the context of our particular university.

We were grateful for time to be creative and to reflect on themes related to women's leadership and leadership aspirations. We fully expected to draft a book proposal that weekend. A weekend retreat would provide an island of time in which to accomplish this; it would provide a moment of freedom in which to clear our heads of the distractions of daily life and the nuances of academia. We did not, however, anticipate the lasting effect that the weekend would have on each of us individually and on our developing identity and cohesiveness as a group. Embedded in the narratives that we shared at the retreat were themes of women navigating their world, and the very personal challenges and obstacles that each encountered along the way. The narratives described the career trajectory and unique pathway to leadership experienced by each of the women in our group. We shared our stories and received the stories of our colleagues with understanding and empathy. We could feel our group identity growing stronger and more coherent as a result of sharing and listening deeply.

During that memorable weekend in 2016 members of the group shared their lived experiences and in that process several themes related to our individual feminist pathways to leadership emerged. The narratives that we shared were rich with examples of determination and resolve defining the life and career trajectory of academic women. These personal narratives included the many unique and unexpected pathways leading to roles that encompass a range of non-traditional definitions of leadership. The oral narratives served as the impetus for our group to delve into the process of defining alternative forms that leadership can embody, particularly for women striving to rise above the many societal and cultural barriers that they encountered along the way.

As each member shared their story, we collected topics and themes that were repeated in each story. We could clearly see themes that were evolving that shaped each member's leadership identity development journey. As the member of LEAD who facilitated the activity, I had the privilege of asking questions to elaborate on themes while other members acted as note-takers. As we nourished ourselves in this cozy inn with food and wine and shared our very personal stories, we experienced why a group like LEAD is important and can't be contained in a workshop series with the same results.

Our narratives spoke of the gendered experiences of women in their leadership journey that were not new to the research literature particularly in women's leadership development but spoke to the need for an understanding of the lived experience across women's identities of these themes. These themes created an authentic framework for our book proposal and are more fully developed by the authors within the subsequent chapters.

Caretaking

Each member represented relationships and caretaking in their maps and spoke about them in their stories – relationships with childhood families; partners and spouses, children, grandchildren, siblings, and colleagues. We spoke about how caretaking in these relationships impacted career choices, opportunities, and fields of study. Since our group spanned a wide age range, we spoke about the impact of caretaking at different stages from infancy to aging parents and health challenges in families. Most

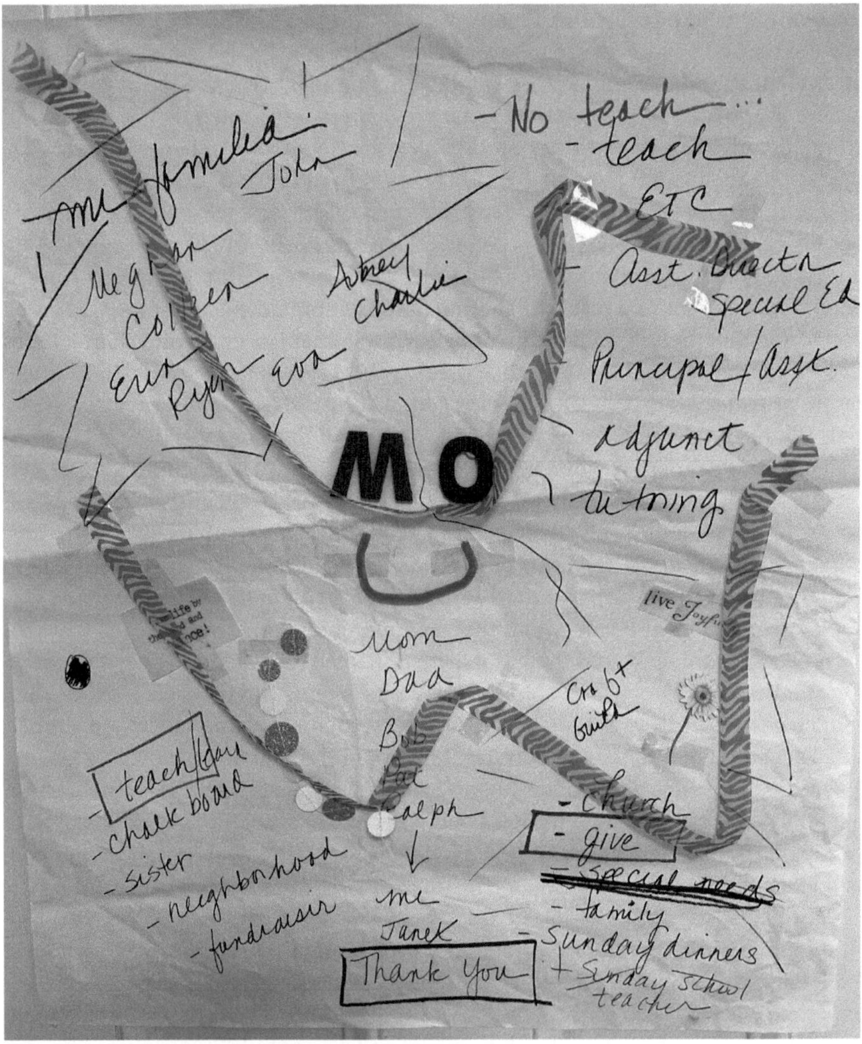

Figure 2.2 Gail's heart shows her identity as mother and family relationships as central to her journey.

members shared stories where they had to say no to an opportunity because of family demands or a "hold my breath and just do it" moment all the while hoping for the best as they took on a new challenge. Our lived experiences were examples of what the research literature has long documented – women have an additional contextual factor in their leadership development that are not accounted for in traditional leadership development models – family responsibilities (Seltzer, 2015).

Obstacles and Barriers

Many participants intermixed stories of leadership experiences with challenges they faced, even from a young age. Almost every member started their stories

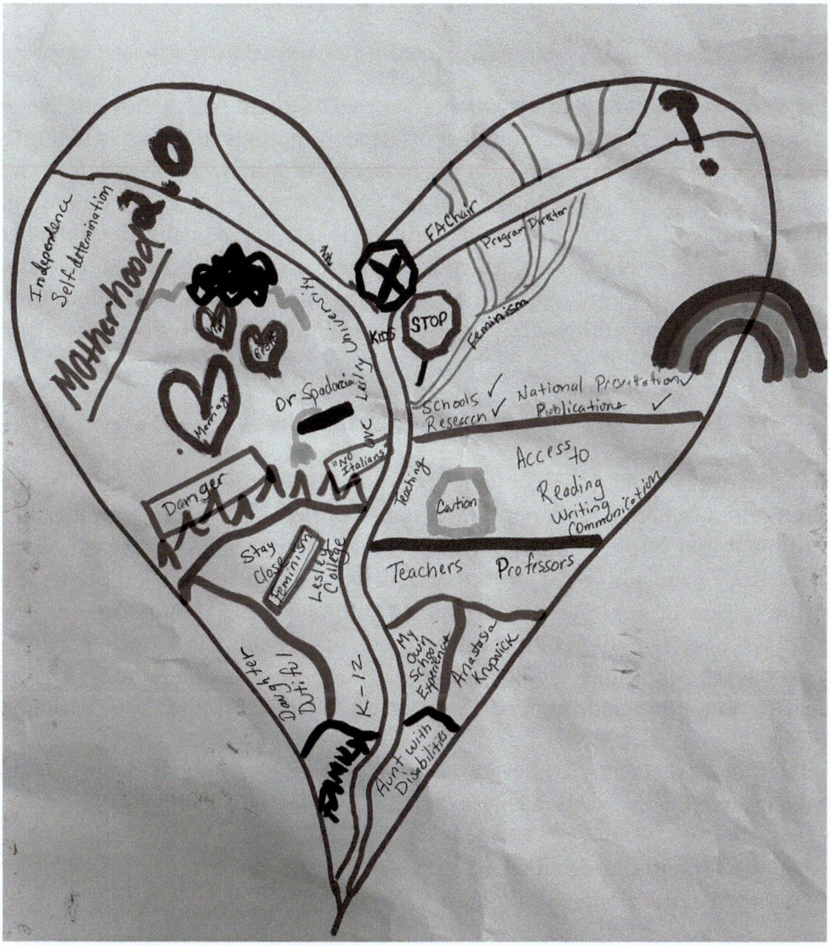

Figure 2.3 Stephanie's heart showing her journey and balance between personal and professional life and the barriers she experienced.

with their childhood homes and families and how class, socioeconomic status, and other expectations based on assumptions of identity impacted the choices they made. Some spoke about how going to college was an expectation and a priority in the family while others spoke about gendered expectations of college and career paths such as going into a helping profession or one that would have a flexible schedule in order to be a mother. As Chapter 1 described the group's membership and the relative homogeneity of the racial and ethnic make-up of the group, the members were acutely aware of barriers they faced and how they would differ for women from different identity groups – therefore not making assumptions about the experiences of women not present at the retreat or in the LEAD group process ["just add women and stir" in order to have leadership equilibrium]. Not all women face the same obstacles and barriers in their leadership identities.

Male-Dominated Contexts

Many stories highlighted an experience (or two or three) where they challenged expectations based on assumptions of gender in male dominated contexts. Within the context of higher education, most opportunities for advancement rely on heavy scholarship, "public or perish," and extensive university community service – both of which assume that there are no other responsibilities outside of the job. Several of our colleagues spoke of feeling forced to say yes to leading a committee or task force as it would advance their career and standing in the community, knowing full well that they were leading other initiatives as well and the time burden would be significant.

Invitations to Lead

One consistent point in each member's story was that moment where they were invited to take a leadership role, made a brave choice and took a risk, or were mentored into a leadership role. Some stories included disaster stories where things did not go well, either through perceived lack of preparation for the role or through lack of support to fully enact the role. Along the way, most members named mentors and sponsors that supported them in particular ways – teachers, senior faculty, administrators, or outside mentors. The impact of mentorship and models of leadership on other women was formative for many.

The themes that emerged from this activity were far-ranging and represent the challenges and women in leadership face including the following:

- Building from failure and challenges
- Guiding the development of others

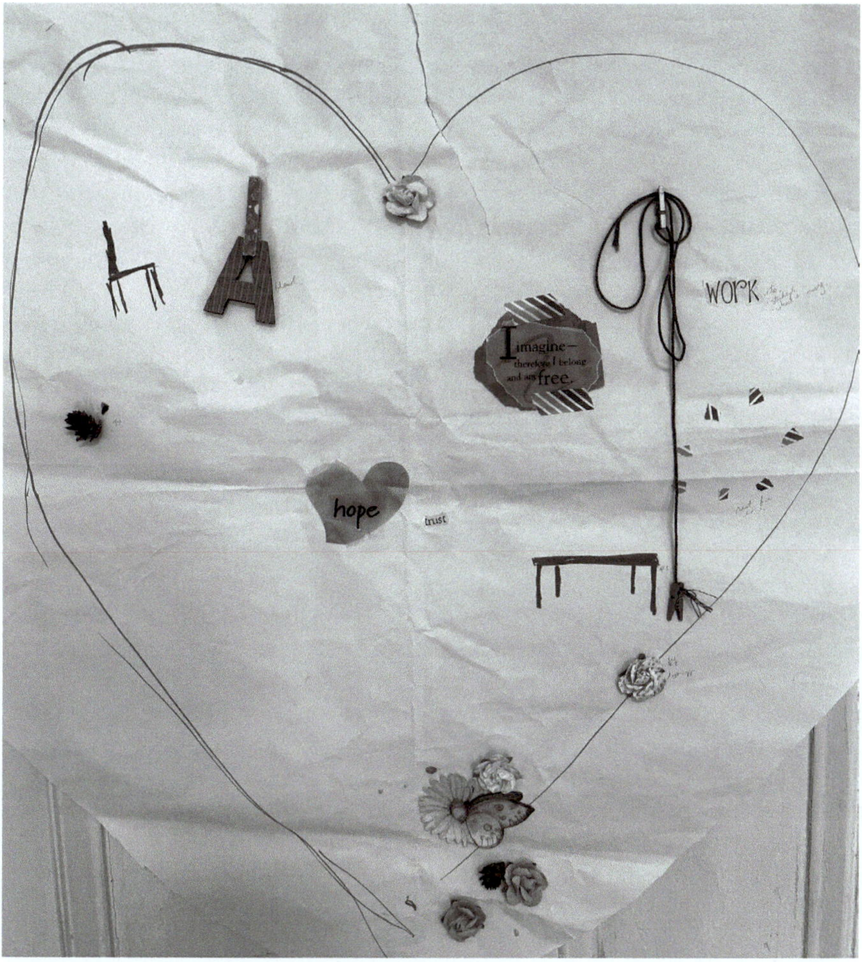

Figure 2.4 Diana's heart showing an image of a chair, representing a pivotal moment in her professional career.

- Are collaborative leaders perceived as weaker in settings?
- Social class and mothering
- Imposter syndrome
- Balancing the work of a particular role with our own leadership development
- Evaluation of leadership in different cultures and contextual settings

Reflective Retrospective on Leadership Identity Development

In the fall of 2020, the writing was still in progress and individual chapters were in draft form. It seemed like an opportune time to take stock of the personal and professional experiences that were shaping or reshaping the views of LEAD members regarding self, society, and more current understandings related to leadership. I wanted to think about how being a part of a peer and self-mentoring group had been influential on the personal leadership development of each member. At my request, the smaller subgroup (the women who were able to remain committed to writing this book and who became the core of our peer group during the pandemic) repeated the heart mapping exercise during a virtual meeting that fateful summer of 2020. We agreed that this moment in time would be conducive to rethinking and sharing more current understandings related to leadership from a feminist perspective, especially against the backdrop of our changing society.

Interviews

To better understand the leadership development of women in LEAD I conducted in-depth individual interviews with five volunteers; women who participated in the follow-up heart mapping activity and were willing to delve into self-reflection during the interview process. I wanted to create portrayals of feminist leadership development that encompassed a sampling of the varying stages of career trajectories within the group, and of course, I needed to consider the willingness of the volunteers to share the intimacies of their personal and professional journey.

The interviews lasted for approximately one hour each. The interviews felt personal, revealing, and gave me a sense of the beautiful essence of each of my colleagues: as a person, as a woman, and as a leader. I felt a strong responsibility to capture each woman authentically. I wanted my portrayals to be accurate. I read and reread the transcribed interviews to seek out the dominant themes that appeared within and across the narratives. To create interrater reliability, my peer editor and colleague examined the interview data and provided thoughtful input regarding the emerging themes within each interview. I asked the interviewees to read the portrayal or snapshot that I had written to summarize the data, and explained my willingness to edit the content in cases where I may have misrepresented, or details that the interviewee preferred not to make public. As it turned out there were very few examples of these changes.

These interviews include reflections on the heart mapping that took place during our 2016 retreat in the sea captain's home and some comparisons with the data derived from more recent mapping and sharing. While the interviews began with reflections of the original shared experience they extended beyond that one moment in time that we had captured so well so long ago. In a sense, the stories of my colleagues collectively weave a tapestry depicting the powerful impact of each woman's lived experiences, their evolving conceptualizations of leadership, and how participation in a critical feminist peer and self-mentoring group has been influential to the development of each as a leader in academia.

The Data

To tell the story of the leadership identity journey of my colleagues with authenticity and to seek out recurring themes across the narratives, I refer to: (a) Original heart maps that were produced at the 2016 retreat; (b) New heart maps that were created during the virtual follow-up meeting that took place in summer of 2020; and (c) interviews conducted virtually during the summer and fall of 2020. Each participant was asked these four questions:

- Can you put yourself back into the weekend four years ago and recall any of the sights or sounds of our shared retreat?
- What do you recall about the heart mapping activity?
- What do you recall about reflecting on your life experiences and leadership identity journey of sharing your native with the group?
- Can you recall any experiences in LEAD that were particularly meaningful to you?

The Lived Experiences

As you prepare to read the five portraits featured below, think about how these women understand and carry out their leadership roles. Consider their lived experiences and the ways that experience has shaped perceptions of self as women and as leaders. Also think about participation in LEAD, a peer and self-mentoring critical feminist group, and how the group has facilitated the development of beliefs and practices regarding leadership. The pronouns that are used in the portrait descriptions reflect the preferred pronouns of the participants.

The narratives of Amy and Diana are presented first. Both are in the mid-career phase of leadership. They are trained respectively in public health and social sciences and psychology, professors and leaders in an academic setting. These narratives will be followed by those of Gail, Stephanie and Barbara, ranging in mid- to mature-phases of their career, accomplished educators and professors in the same academic setting.

Amy, to be introduced first, holds an important leadership position in a graduate school of education. Her narrative, featured below as *Portrait #1* captures reflections of her journey leading up to this current position. Amy's reflections (as well as the others that follow) are contextualized within a backdrop of a nation and a university whose population was anxious with regard to a raging pandemic and reacting to a long overdue reckoning with racial injustice. As educators and educational leaders, our university colleagues carried (and still carry) the weight of their own circumstances, the circumstances of the graduate students and in-service teachers who are degree candidates and the PreK-12 children who are their students. Amy has stepped into a challenging leadership role that bears all the weightiness of the moment. We can see that Amy reflected on her identity as a leader in a challenging role.

Portrait #1

Amy: Nurturing Others

> *I bring my whole self into my leadership caring about others and advocating for their professional and personal well-being.*

Recalling the first weekend retreat that we experienced as a group, Amy shared that it felt warm and comfortable inside, although raw, cold and rainy outside. The heart mapping activity was a provocative experience that was powerful enough to generate rich content and reflection in a relatively short timeframe. Some of us knew each other, but some of us didn't know each other at all; and yet:

> Being able to go so deep so quickly was actually a jarring experience and no one anticipated that the data would be ripe on so many levels: personal, cultural, historical, sociopolitical and gendered. The space, the time, the group all came together to set the conditions to go deep that weekend. We were sitting on the cusp of the 2016 presidential election, excited, full of anticipation and awaiting the moment when we would learn that Hillary was our new president! In retrospect, if we had anticipated what was to unfold we would have had cameras ready to record the stories that unfolded – profound reflections on the lived experiences of women over time.

Amy's map reflected three key formative elements to her leadership development. First, was her family's viewpoint that she could achieve without parameters. Another important influence were her feelings of responsibility as a caregiver in her family: "I know I very much internalized caregiving expectations and responsibilities at an early age, which very much influenced my paths." A third was the mentoring and sponsorship that she received early in their career. All of these elements shaped the strong relational-cultural paradigm that this woman believes shaped her current work as a leader, professor, and scholar.

At 23 years old, and in a doctoral program at Columbia University, Amy's father became ill, resulting in the need for leave of absence. During that year a position became available at a small private college, and she was hired as full-time faculty. Even though she was very young, she recalled that her leadership potential was recognized, and several new opportunities were made available to her. Her father's illness and the need to stay home to help her mother with her younger brother resulted in her decision to stay with the position in the small private college for a longer time than she had originally anticipated. During that time period she developed a counseling center for the college. This is significant in that Amy identified a need and took appropriate action to fill that need, a particularly feminist stance to take in terms of service and responsivity to the needs of others.

Amy recalled opportunities that resulted from relationships with the many mentors and sponsors that supported her along the way, opportunities that helped her grow as a leader in the roles that she was fortunate enough to fill. She subsequently became chair of the Liberal Studies Department at the same small college, and later the Vice President asked her to do research to develop health professions programming. She ultimately became the founding director of the Allied Health Division. All of this, she stated, was the result of an unbelievable set of opportunities created by mentors who "Plucked me up, sponsored me, and gave me opportunities to create." She attributes the mentorship and sponsorship that she received to be a thread that allowed her to move ahead, and it is a thread that she traced as she reflected on their personal leadership map, extending onward to the next career step at Massachusetts General Hospital. It was there that she got to know the Dean and President and their mentoring was most beneficial to her development as a leader. Ultimately, Amy found her way to complete the doctorate that she had begun some years earlier. Again, there were many mentors; women and men who recognized her inherent potential and encouraged her as a doctoral student.

Amy reflects on the courage it takes to be open, caring, and even vulnerable at times: "I really try to listen to keep my mind open and really hear the point of view being expressed. When people enter the dialogue with aggression or a harsh tone it becomes hard to listen, to lean in with openness and curiosity." She went on to say "I am not the smartest person in the room, but I bring my whole self into the leadership role. I care and worry about my colleagues, and I lead from a caring position."

To that point, this leader has extended herself to protect faculty during times of budget deficits and reports that she "deeply worries about the health of colleagues, especially at this current time when health is a major threat to our nation and to our community." The focus on health and job security of colleagues has been a major defining force. She sees herself at a stark crossroad at this current moment, reflecting deeply on the career pathway of her future and balancing how much she can continue to give without leaving a deficit in their own health and well-being. She is driven by their desire to support the community that she has come to love so deeply.

One of the founding members of our group, Amy believes that the power of LEAD is that it is about mutuality and growth, relationships and connections. Not just for herself, but for all the members and facilitators.

> I think for me it's just been a really safe space to find connection and support, to help others grow and to help myself grow. So, you know, I mean, I think the power of LEAD is that it's inherently about mutuality. I mean leaders have grown, the facilitators have grown, all of us have grown in different ways by being together in this space. And really wonderful relationships have been forged; friendships, connections. But I think, but I think inherently that I have seen us all grow: Every single member that has stayed in I have seen grow both professionally and personally and in their scholarship, and each has found voice in their own way.

Amy believes that this process is replicable in other spaces and in other institutions. She is dedicated to mutual leadership development from a feminist perspective. She advocates for supporting the group we call LEAD.

Looking at Amy's current heart map we can see the centrality of courage within the turbulence of the moment, and branches of a tree within her map leading to collaboration, empathy, relationships, and self.

Amy: Summative Comments

Amy's focus on *social relational leadership* has certainly been evident in the ways she has carried out the many facets of the leadership role. Amy gained the confidence of colleagues through tireless efforts and *service to others* at times when job security was in peril and when health and safety were a concern for many colleagues. She continued to be a strong collegial advocate over time.

Other experiences such as the strong and effective *mentors and sponsors* who recognized her potential and created opportunities throughout her career pathway made a positive difference. These experiences were reflected in her willingness to be a mentor to and a sponsor for others.

Amy found herself in a demanding leadership position even though it may not have been what she had planned for at the moment. She was asked to fill an immediate need resulting from a vacancy at the time. Her *humility and vulnerability* were displayed in her courage to open herself up to others and really hear what colleagues have to say, even when it is difficult.

This leader presents a portrait of a feminist who is focused on nurturing others. The challenge for Amy is refilling her personal well of self-nourishment. Is it possible to give so much of yourself without finding a way to recharge? Amy demonstrated this characteristic of her leadership through a disposition to care for, listen to, and advocate for colleagues, especially during a stressful time within our university, resulting from a pandemic and changes within the greater society. Amy's reflections remind us of the sacrifices one makes when operating in a relational leadership space, especially as a self-identified woman.

Portrait #2

Diana: Advocate and Provider of Information

> *My service to others includes keeping people informed and connected, providing accurate information, and communicating with those who are not currently at the table.*

Diana felt lucky to be part of that weekend with all of us. She didn't feel particularly well that weekend and had to work on staying focused. The call from home and her need to mediate an interaction between husband and 11-year-old son were somewhat of a temporary distraction, but she pushed on. She recalled the unique beauty of the inn: the old creaky staircase leading up and down, tree branches draped across the ceiling in the great room, and the small trinket that she admired, a sparkly apple. She felt happy that the arts and crafts materials that she brought with her were being used by everyone to create their heart maps.

She wasn't sure about her legitimacy as a leader in the sense that her pathway hadn't included any formal leadership positions. She saw herself as an observer of leadership as carried out by others and felt that her perceptions of leadership were gained vicariously by observing others. Diana's participation in the heart activity, as she recalled, was guided more by her observational experiences than by reflections on her own leadership experiences. She watched everyone else "dive in," using the craft materials that she provided, but could not help but think, "OK, here I am with nothing to share about my own journey, will my representations be completely real?" The heart map that was created, as she described it to me during the interview, had small stories, not necessarily woven together to represent a clear journey or pathway. She recalled that as she created her heart, she used chairs in their artistic depictions: chairs at the table, an anecdote regarding an executive director at a previous job, who sat on the floor rather than taking a chair from others around the table. This seemed meaningful to Diana because she interpreted this as an example of a servant leader for whom it was more important for others to have a chair rather than herself.

As this participant listened to her colleagues present, she was touched by the disclosures and frustrated by the need to hold back comments or perspectives (as a trained therapist). She noted that for many of the women sharing their experiences, being invited to fill a leadership role was more common than competing and being selected.

Thinking about her leadership journey, Diana recalled the negative experience of competing for and not being selected for a leadership position that she applied for within the institution during the years after the original retreat. She found the experience to be "devastating and hurtful," but as these things often do, it turned out for the best, leading to her current leadership position. Looking back, however, she realizes that she successfully formed relationships that were mutually beneficial and believes that these relationships have facilitated success in her current leadership role.

Diana describes her leadership as service to others. The service includes keeping people informed and connected, providing accurate information, and communicating with those who are not currently at the table. She feels that having correct information relieves or prevents anxiety that faculty may feel in time of change with many unknowns. Part of keeping people informed, she relates, "Is providing a bigger picture to the conversation." By this she means that the "Actions people take are not generally isolated, but that systems work together like 'cogs and wheels.' Actions have consequences and understanding the bigger picture often prevents unintended consequences. If people understand the bigger picture, they often shift to encompass different, or alternative ways of thinking."

When thinking about the influence of the LEAD group, Diana expressed how transformative and loving it has been to be enveloped by a group who sees her so differently than she sees herself. A group that challenges her to reach her potential as a leader. The relationships have meant so much to her. She doesn't know what her leadership future will look like. Her current role feels like a good fit for now, Diana expresses her gratitude and says she feels supported by those around her. She cannot envision herself in a new place or a new role.

Diana: Summative Comments

Like the subject of the first portrait, Diana is a LEAD group facilitator, similarly in a mid-career phase, who has risen to a position of leadership in academia. Diana's leadership narrative is another quintessential story, highlighting leadership development from a feminist perspective.

Diana defines herself as one who serves others and places the needs of others first. At the retreat she was ready to supportively address the emotional needs expressed by others, especially when listening to aspects of the narratives shared. Yet she called into question her own narrative, her own "legitimacy" as a leader, and even described feelings of "failure" and "devastation" at challenging pivotal moments in her career. Diana expressed the emotions of feeling vulnerability and shame, as well as gratitude: emotions that can be aligned with positive professional and personal development as a leader and demonstrate to others how a woman in leadership may successfully grapple with and rise above challenges.

In her role, and consistent with her orientation to providing for others, she is often in the position of explaining policies to faculty members. She believes that accurate information is a crucial element in achieving harmony, especially in a time of change and uncertainty within the university, and certainly in light of the misinformation that was currently spiraling (and continues) across our nation at the time. Diana tries to help her colleagues by providing accurate and up to date information, helping others and seeing the bigger picture when policy concerns are brought forward. Being a liaison between colleagues and university administrators can be wrought with challenge, yet she serves primarily as an advocate for colleagues. *The leadership role Diana currently occupies is that of an advocate and a provider of information regarding administrative policy and practice.*

Portrait #3

Gail: Connecting, Including, and Providing Opportunities for Others

> *"Leadership is a set of attributes rather than a title. Regardless of the role you fill you can demonstrate leadership."*

Gail recalled the retreat weekend with vivid memories of the amazing location by the sea, of the walks we took, of the food, and trying a *Moscow Mule* for the first time! She recalled the heart mapping activity and the ways that she was introspective about her experiences, taking herself all the way back to when she was just 9 years old. She recalled how advocacy for her younger sister made an impact in her sister's educational placement. She also recalled how, as a child, she created a school in her parent's garage, and how neighborhood children were clamoring to get in, because even as a child she recognized that acknowledging the good efforts of others could make a positive impact. Children who seemed to be trying and were attempting to complete their "assignments" were rewarded with a seat in a chaise lounge at the front of the make-shift classroom in the garage. She rotated turns each day to ensure that all students were rewarded with a seat in the special chair.

Gail's recollections of the retreat were vivid: How evocative it was to make use of the arts and crafts materials used to create the heart maps – bringing back images of her mother, a seamstress, always sewing and crocheting, and how sharing her narrative and listening to others in the group seemed to occur within a "circle of trust" that made her feel safe. In her words, the feeling of unity became solidified during that weekend. She recalled how she appreciated the feedback she received at the time, and captured the essence of the LEAD group by saying that others in our group recognized the importance of what she had shared publicly and acknowledged her value as a woman and as a human being. She expressed the idea that the experience *crystalized* the notion that our group would continue to be a safe place for sharing. She felt supported. She felt that it was like "a big group therapy experience."

Gail didn't relate any one particular pivotal experience, but rather a series of experiences that reinforced her ideas regarding leadership. She indicated that leadership was not necessarily a title or a role, but rather that leadership was demonstrated in the behaviors of the individual. She expanded on this by saying that regardless of the role you fill, you can demonstrate leadership. She clarified that she believed you can be a leader in any role, as she has been, working to better an organization, supporting people in meaningful ways, and building trusting relationships.

Gail provided examples gleaned from many situations along the journey of her career. Beginning with her successful schoolhouse at 9 years old, and again during their high school and college years Gail took on challenges at every point to work with teachers and school administrators to share her work to benefit her field of study. Gail expressed the notion of leadership as building the structures and setting the climate in which individuals and organizations can grow. Ultimately, throughout her 30 years as an educator, Administrator of Special Education, and Assistant Principal in a large city in Massachusetts she developed group structures for collaboration among classroom teachers and specialists and established much needed programming for special education services and reading intervention. She reflected with pride on being able to balance the complexities of relationships between schools, teachers, parents and other stakeholders in the special education process. She attributes this to her ability to build trusting cultures and create structures that included many voices. This practice established Gail as a leader with a commitment to inclusive equity on many levels, true for educators as well as children.

Gail was the Faculty Assembly chair at her university, and there too, she worked to establish the much-needed structures that would serve to benefit the organization. She restructured the use of time, creating small groups that were amenable to encouraging even less vocal faculty to express their opinions and suggestions or ask questions in a smaller, more comfortable space. She organized the agenda setting, cleaned up the record keeping of committees, and acknowledged the value of each committee's contribution to university governance. She made time on the agenda for each of the committees to contribute. She institutionalized the use of *Exit tickets* to ensure that the voices of all faculty were heard, highlighting their feminist relational stance as a faculty leader.

Gail: Summative Comments

Membership in LEAD was an affirmation for Gail. It affirmed what she knew intuitively about being a feminist leader and gave her the language with which to talk about it. Even within her doctoral studies in Educational Leadership most concepts were presented from the perspective of men in leadership. There was limited exposure to leadership through a feminine lens.

Her years as a member of this feminist group informed her and helped her to think about and talk about issues of women in positions of leadership as she engaged with others in the group. LEAD gave her support, friendship, and courage.

It enabled her to move ahead with more confidence. Gail hopes to seek out other opportunities for leadership and service within the university.

Gail defines leadership as a set of behaviors rather than a title or the authority that accompanies it. She believes that anyone can be a leader. A teacher at heart, Gail began at an early age setting up a school in her garage (finding ways to be affirmative to students, even then), and continued throughout her career as an activist, a contributor, and builder of supportive structures. Her focus is on inclusivity and welcoming many participants to the table.

Now at the mature stage of career trajectory, she has successfully demonstrated leadership in numerous roles. It was the LEAD group that gave her the language to express the concerns and nuances of leadership from a feminist stance and put words to what she already knew intuitively: supporting others, building trusting and positive relationships.

Portrait #4

Stephanie: True Leadership Involves Inclusion, Advocacy, and Voice

> *I used to think that feminism and leadership equaled being heard. But being heard does not necessarily mean increasing the volume.*

Stephanie put herself back in that room, into the time and the place. She remembered images: the long bar, the evening, food, lots of small spaces, a long table, couches, trees, and beautiful light streaming through windows in the morning. It was a cold weekend, as she recalled. She said that she thought, "We all felt bonded together in our creativity that evening and into the next day." She herself felt excited to create and share a representation of her journey, by a road beginning as a young college student, then teacher, mother, and now an academic. Her road was a crooked one, with the left side depicting personal events and the right side professional. Her map had many cracks in the road or obstacles to overcome, highlighting the tension women feel to balance family life and obligations with career.

Some things on the left and right sides came together in the heart map. She remembered how much she wanted to be a teacher, and her father, but did not object to her desired pathway: "Because teachers had flexibility and time off in the summer to raise a family." Stephanie expressed the culturally embedded perception that is a common theme for women in career development: the need to be a mother and a nurturer as a life priority.

In addition, a history of a family member with long term illness and disability, as well as generational family mental health challenges influenced her desire to become a special educator. She always felt herself to be a strong advocate for individuals with learning challenges, to aspire toward reading and writing proficiency, and to consider herself to be a champion of literacy.

Stephanie knew she wanted to attend an all-women undergraduate college and she was influenced by the climate of the university setting at that time, very influenced by the female university president who served as a role model for her. The influence of this president's leadership served as a model that awakened her thinking about the power and potential of women in leadership. Stephanie's experience at the university at the time was one of social awareness and recognition of injustices. She moved on to advance her education at a prestigious university in the south, returning home to her undergraduate alma mater to continue on a career pathway as a professor in teacher education focused on special education and literacy instruction.

Her professional years as an educator were extremely influential in developing awareness of feminism as an influential force. Her zigzagging pathway came together at a pivotal time, with two children to support she needed to divert her pathway away from academic writing and national presentations. Although leadership aspirations were always present, she needed to direct her attention to her children, and her parents. While still a relatively new faculty member when she began a family, she continued to develop a career while supporting two children, ultimately as a single parent. Stephanie once again highlighted the sociocultural tension between family caretaking, both of children and aging parents, while attending to important opportunities for career development, such as national presentations and conferences that require time away from home and family.

With respect to leadership development, Stephanie recalls what it has been like on the pathway. She recalls the "crack in the road" created by the *"man-splaining"* she experienced along the way, highlighting the dominant culture of male correctness and the silencing of the voices of women. *"If a man said it, the idea was accepted,"* often demonstrating "disregard for a woman's place at the table." Stephanie was aware of the dominance of male voices that was often demonstrated at meetings, but did not have an official name for it, or more importantly, a confirmation that other women also recognized and were troubled by this inequity. The LEAD group helped Stephanie to find her own voices in male dominated environments.

Stephanie feels a strong desire to build trusting relationships with her colleagues based upon her personal understanding of faculty life. As a rising leader and single mom, she feels herself pulled in many directions with a more than full-time job and children at home. In her ear she hears: *"Kids, dishes, meetings, got to go home and make dinner."* As the years passed, she became chair of the Faculty Assembly, her first real leadership position as recognized by the university structure that was in place at the time. In subsequent leadership positions as program director and department chair, Associate Dean, and currently Vice-Provost, Stephanie aspires to express empathy and to support work and life balance for members of her department, thus highlighting her focus on leadership from a feminist, relational perspective. She especially wonders how to support more diverse faculty leaders, across different intersections of race, gender identity, ability, language and culture, to acknowledge cultural differences, and make sure everyone has a seat at the table.

Many self-identified women experienced similar barriers created by male interpretations of leadership and the deficits attributed to career women aspiring to fill leadership roles. In retrospect, she stated emphatically, "My map would look different now. My pathway would demonstrate that as an educator and as an advocate for students I was already demonstrating leadership." Like so many of the LEAD members, Stephanie did not fully recognize her leadership identity with a voice and agency prior to joining the group. Stephanie's narrative once again highlights the power of the LEAD group and the ways that group participation has served to advance the leadership identity of its members.

In comparing the heart map created during the summer of 2020 with the original one, Stephanie is prompted to think about her evolution. I used to think that feminism and leadership equaled being heard. But being heard, as she now better understands, does not necessarily mean increasing the volume. It is much more than, *"I am women, hear me roar,"* rather authentic and beneficial feminist leadership has more to do with relational leadership.

Stephanie concluded that leadership means the merging of self and others to build, define, and construct. "Leadership is not hierarchical, that the leader is not necessarily at the top of the map, that it is centered and nuanced and other-focused." Going forward Stephanie wants to move ahead on an administrative trajectory when the time is right for her. She still has a long time ahead in her working life and is contemplating choices that will make sense.

Stephanie: Summative Comments

Stephanie presents as a striver in the face of challenges: a caretaker for older parents, her sibling, and young children. Early on, the mental health concerns of family members shaped her desire to be an educator, specifically a teacher educator in Special Educator and Literacy. Later, as a single mom and caregiver, she was immersed in balancing the many responsibilities of career and motherhood. She experienced obstacles presented by male colleagues, none-the-less her journey led to a more authentic conceptual understanding of her leadership identity. Having a strong model of a feminist leader provided inspiration, and she used all of her experiences to help re-define and expand conceptions related to authentic leadership.

Stephanie has come to see that leadership encompasses many actions: her previous advocacy for young students, and her current advocacy for colleagues. She came to an understanding that being heard grew from connections with others, rather than the volume of her voice. She began to understand that leadership entailed a shifting emphasis from self to others and to see to it that all of her colleagues have an authentic voice. When the time is right, this woman feels that she will be prepared to move into new leadership roles.

Portrait #5

Barbara: Increasing Scope of Influence and Self-Confidence as a Leader

> *My professional growth has not been one pivotal event, rather a series of things, each experience leading to the next.*

Barbara recalled the musty smell. She loved the furniture; took snapshots of the unusual nautical themed décor. She was happy and full of anticipation that weekend. She knew some of the women fairly well, and others were less familiar to her. When the narratives were shared, she felt a kind of "awe" for the sharers and all they had experienced as aspirational women leading up to this very moment. She could recall the "hubbub" of activity in every room during the preparation phase when the heart maps were being created. Women in every room working with glue, art supplies, and poster paper. She recalled the snacks. She loved being with women in education, sharing, talking, and embarking on the unknown together. It felt exciting.

Barbara wasn't sure what she had to offer at that moment in time because she felt that she had limited leadership experience, but nonetheless, she began reflecting and creating her map. In her original map created that weekend in 2016, she portrayed their life as she saw it, "not a big life, but a nice life," filled with family, and the things she enjoyed, like hiking and kayaking, travel, camping, and her role in her synagogue. She realized that she had, at that time, forgotten about significant experiences such as her professional affiliations in special education, professional leadership roles, consultancies, directorships, articles, and presentations.

When asked about pivotal events, Barbara told me that writing her Annual Faculty Report, prompted her into a reflective mode and made her realize that she had begun to carry out many leadership activities. She came to the realization that each activity of leadership was a learning experience that helped her grow as a leader, and she believed that the skills she acquired carried over from one context to another. For example, taking on a temple leadership role in adult education and serving as the chair of a faculty scholarship committee at the university mutually informed each other. Likewise, being on a university search committee and on a synagogue search committee simultaneously demonstrated that her leadership skills in one setting reinforced similar skills in the other. Barbara participated in two high ranking service committees at the university, thus building self-confidence. Within her temple community, she facilitated conversations and trained other facilitators for an interfaith community alliance, a position for which she felt ready when asked to lead. She described her progression as a leader as moving through a funnel in reverse direction, narrow at the beginning and widening at the end.

Barbara highlights her feminist relational leadership stance as she describes her development as a leader, reaffirming the false premise that embodies traditional notions of leadership. "My professional growth has not been one pivotal event, rather a series of things, each experience leading to the next." She told me that she grew in confidence as she began to gain competencies. "I always listened," she said,

> And worked to improve relationship building, tried to really know other people, to be of service, to match people with others who could help them, and I became better and better at these things as I grew. I never wanted to become the director of my program, but once in the role I grew into the role, seeking information, collaborating with colleagues, and gaining more and more agency.

As we looked at Barbara's newer heart map (Figure 2.5), recreated as a LEAD group activity during the summer of the pandemic in 2020, and compared it with the original heart map (on the right, below) created at the retreat of fall 2016, we see a more developed depiction of herself as a leader. She depicts the building blocks of leadership as she experienced them, leading her to the broader characteristics of relational leadership, including empathy, communication, service, and risk taking.

The group has been influential for Barbara. It helped her realize that the perception of true leaders as highly confident, competent, and full of certainty was probably false. She saw that the others in the group had to work out uncertainties, and that as a group we could mutually support one another in this process. "It is no coincidence," Barbara indicated, "that over the years together our group members have taken on a range of leadership positions within the university."

She looks backward over her long and productive career, and muses that when she was younger, she wanted to become an extraordinary teacher, "*The-Best-Teacher-in-the-World*," but wound up making her contribution to the profession in a different way:

> Maybe it is not exactly what I had hoped for, but in some ways it was all good, and real. I've made contributions to my university, and I am proud of the students I send out into the profession. I am proud of the teachers I prepare, and I feel that the future is wide open for my students and for myself.

Barbara realizes that her contributions to education have been significant. Barbara looks ahead as well, thinking of new leadership opportunities in the next phase of her life.

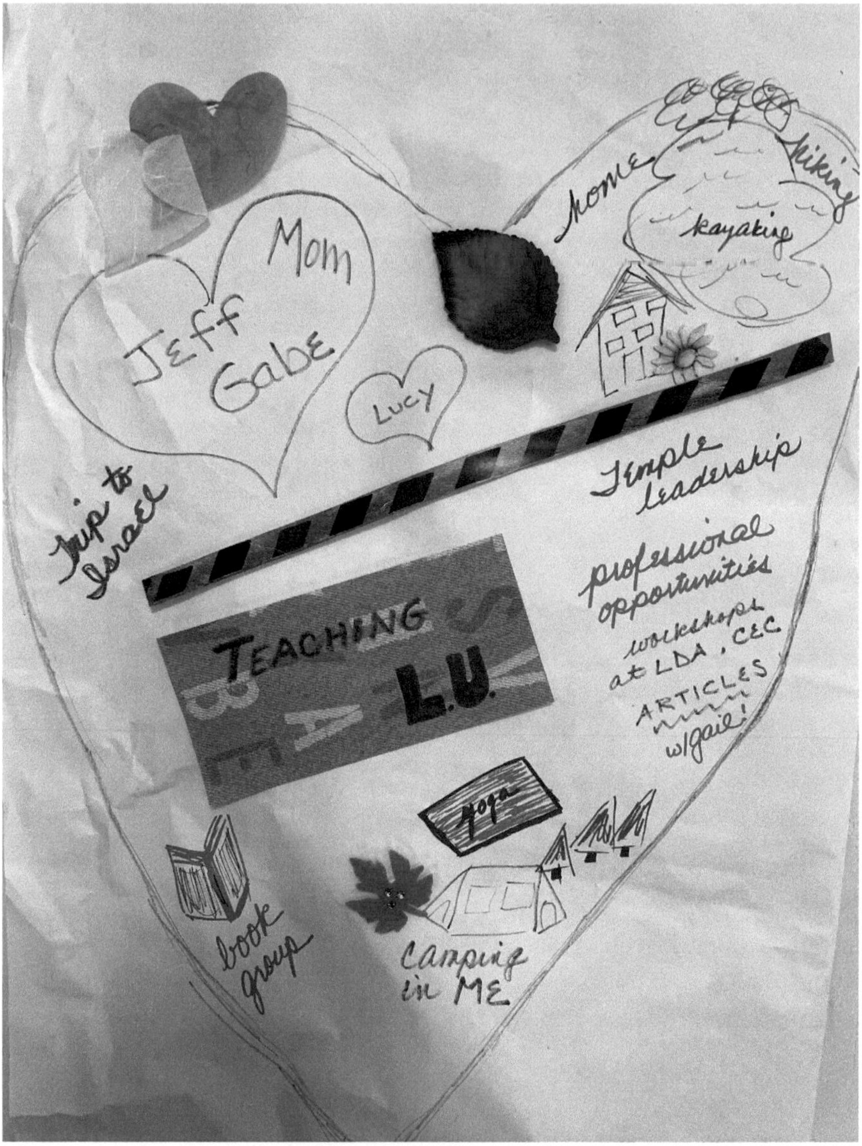

Figure 2.5 Barbara's heart showing her self-realization of leadership developing.

Barbara: Summative Comments

At every step along the way, Barbara took advantage of opportunities and made connections that helped her acquire skills and apply them in other, newer contexts. She had self-doubt about her leadership experiences – or maybe it was the trait of modesty and humility (so often attributed to feminine characteristics) that caused Barbara to momentarily forget all that she had contributed to her professional associations. *She grew into leadership in academia with the help of sister LEAD members, who made her realize that some occasional uncertainty and self-doubt were probably more accurate depictions of authentic leaders. Barbara concluded that the notion of a leader as highly confident and full of certainty was probably false.* At the end of her long career, she looks forward and back; thinking about next steps as she reflects on her many accomplishments and what they represent.

Reflections from My Own Heart

I have been given the opportunity to think about and write about each woman and her development as a leader over time. I could not complete this chapter, however, without reflecting on what I have personally learned from the experience. Below are the insights that I personally find most compelling with regard to data that was embedded in the heart maps and interviews.

Leadership is not necessarily constrained by a title. Exemplifications of leadership are captured in the personal attributes and behaviors of women in leadership. Attributes such as altruism can be demonstrated in the advocacy, service, mentoring, and inclusion that feminist leaders in these portrayals demonstrate with consistency. Women in leadership, as I saw them, often worked from behind the scenes or between the lines, influencing, advocating, modeling, and serving as agents of positive change throughout their career trajectory and at many points along the way in their professional journey. Some of our LEAD members found themselves in positions that they had not asked for when there was a gap that needed to be filled at a specific time. They stepped up and recognized the need to grow into a new leadership role.

For me, I see leadership and leadership development as requiring courage in many forms. One example is the courage to trust. Trust, I believe, grows from lateral, relational leadership. By lateral, I am referring to the collegial interactions and relationships that replace the traditional hierarchical paradigms associated with leadership. None of the interviewees considered herself to be a leader at the top of a hierarchical structure. Their leadership styles, as described, are lateral, other-focused, and relational. They saw themselves predominantly in service to others as their defining leadership quality. Amy enacted this in her keen ability to relate to others, to hear what they say and collaborate to reach solutions. It was through relational interactions that Amy carried out her leadership. Diana was similarly other-focused, seeing her role as a communicator and a clarifier, providing correct and important information to colleagues. She aspired to create an inclusive, collaborative culture, making room for all voices to be heard. Lateral, relational leadership is driven by the establishment of a culture of mutual trust and built on reciprocal relationships; as I see it, trust grows in two (or more) directions. You give trust, and trust is given to you. Reciprocal or relational leadership also focuses on establishing a shared purpose, being inclusive of all voices and distribution of power, in service of producing stronger outcomes.

Based upon my own experiences, and what I have gleaned from these data, a culture of trust creates a space for personal and group growth and development. This was evident in our LEAD group meetings and also evident to me as I combed through the interview data. The courageous leaders that were portrayed here were willing to publicly confront their uncertainty at times, recognize publicly that one person cannot realistically have all of the skills, knowledge, or resources required at any given moment, and demonstrate willingness to model for others the process of collaboration and problem solving.

Another form of courage in leadership that I recognize relates to personal growth and development, self-improvement, and learning. Inherent in learning is self-extension and reaching beyond a comfort zone. It is inherently risky to try something new or challenging because doing so includes the possibility of error. One's vulnerability is on display when stepping onto new, uncharted ground, and the reactions of others may be unknown. How beneficial it can be to let others know that learning is challenging and requires both grit and fortitude.

The attributes of relational, other-focused leadership, and the courage to pursue them with grace, even at challenging moments in a journey toward leadership development; even within organizational structures that may, at times, privilege hierarchical structures and minimize collaborative problem solving have been a great takeaway. I have seen this in the heart maps of the group, and I believe it as well.

Themes Across Portraits

Leadership Identity Development

This group served as a vehicle for its members to co-construct new knowledge, develop self-awareness, and envision identity as leader. It served as a space to probe, extend, and test out understandings with other women striving to develop leadership in an academic setting. We shared the need to shift many of the traditional paradigms related to leadership and learn new ways to conceptualize leadership and new ways to see ourselves within that space. As group members, we acquired the language to talk about leadership through a feminist lens and learned that leaders, especially women in leadership, even accomplished and experienced within their fields are often confronted with uncertainty, vulnerability, and self-doubt.

Clinchy et al. (1996) provided a framework to trace various pathways toward individual leadership development, highlighting the value of a constructivist approach to women's cognitive and leadership development. The authors conducted an extensive interview project involving a diverse group of women and classified participants into a set of cognitive or intellectual stances to describe the ways that women communicate and internalize knowledge. I am including this summary of the research project because it highlights the stance that best describes the discourse patterns and interactions within the LEAD group. Women describe themselves according to the way they engage with others and gain knowledge about the world around them. Women having the ability to listen, share, and cooperate while maintaining their own voice, according to the authors, learn to construct their identity and develop as leaders. This research is significant to the women in the LEAD group because they too have engaged in what Clinchy et al. call "real talk," and it is through this form of authentic discourse that our members have been able to reimagine themselves as leaders in ways that have been relevant to demands of academia and to the world at large.

Courage, Vulnerability, and Grit

The notions of courage, vulnerability, and grit have appeared in several forms within the testimonies of the featured women in this chapter. My colleagues have called into question their own legitimacy, expressed their self-doubt, and even a feeling of shame when career disappointments occurred. They have recognized their own limitations. Yet, for each of the women for whom vulnerability was a strand within their reflections, there was an accompanying expression of the courage they displayed to move forward and serve others as effective leaders.

Brown (2012) supports the claim that vulnerability is a strength and not a weakness. She refers to Theodore Roosevelt's term "daring greatly," as he places the emphasis on leaders who admit errors, take risks, ask for help, and speak the truth. These actions, Brown argues, reflect authenticity and humility. Amy realized that she has much to gain from others and said that she is devoted to listening well. She was courageous enough to bring her whole self to the role, even though she felt vulnerable. Barbara felt her realization that there was great benefit to interactive problem solving within the LEAD group, realizing that it was not authentic to expect leaders to have all the answers all the time. Using vulnerability as an asset, so well described by Brown (2012), and demonstrating the courage to move forward, members of our group have portrayed qualities of leadership from an authentic feminist perspective. We have all come to understand the beneficial process of exposing vulnerabilities as we aspire to become better at what we do, thereby serving as aspirational models for others within the group and beyond.

Societal and Cultural Barriers

Societal and cultural barriers have historically presented obstacles for women. The discussions in our LEAD group helped us better understand traditional, socially ingrained, male-centric assumptions about leadership. For example, interviewees reported the limitations on their career pathway choices based on the expectations of others and their personal sense of responsibility as caretakers. It was normative that responsibility to home and family were seen as the role of women, often leaving many career opportunities open for men, who were for the most part free of similar responsibilities. Hence, leadership positions were predominantly filled by men, perhaps contributing to male-centric conceptions about effective leadership.

Another societal barrier to feminist leaders has been the perspective that leadership is the realm of great men (Mouton, 2019) possessing, if not born with the skills required to lead others.

Such leaders may manage the growth and development of those beneath them in the organizational structure, but even the most positive expression of hierarchical leaders implies raising people up and may be predicated on the notion that the leader resides in a higher place than others. It presumes that he holds most, if not all, of the relevant knowledge and skill, and it is the leader's role to disseminate this capital to others within the organization. The LEAD perspective helped us deconstruct these socially ingrained barriers to women in leadership. We were able to name the obstacles in women's pathway to leadership and experience the ways that self-development was more about facilitating group processes than the leadership skill sets or behaviors of one individual. In many ways, shifting paradigms regarding notions of leadership and leadership development from a male-centric to a critical feminist perspective have been exemplified within the LEAD processes of peer and self-mentoring.

Relational, Other-Centered Leadership

The trait of being other-focused and caring is carried across the women's narratives that have been presented in this chapter. The LEAD group meetings served as a context in which our members could practice and internalize the beneficial process of relationship building, learning, collaboration, and problem solving. Interviewees found the group process to be an asset to their professional growth and self-determination as leaders.

Relational leadership, as exemplified in the portraits of LEAD women, includes caring, responsive leadership, in which the leader is truly responsive to individual colleagues. This is exemplified by listening to what is being said and dedicating energy to caring for others in ways that are authentic and meaningful. The authenticity of caring for others as expressed within interviews distinguished responsive, other-centered leadership from more perfunctory service generally dedicated to serving others, but perhaps restricted to errands or office-related tasks.

Other-centered characteristics such as nurturing, compassion, and humility that have been expressed as overarching themes may stem from early lived experiences as caregivers to siblings, parents, relatives, and more recently to children and other family members. This was expressed within one woman's narrative as their selfless desire to support others in a time of institutional insecurity. It was also represented as making sure others had a seat at the table, and a voice in the conversation. The caring nature of these women leaders may also stem from a stance of being passionate advocates for students, as was the case for educators in the LEAD group who expressed growing understanding regarding advocacy for others, building networks among colleagues, and creating structures for equitable communication as the enactment of leadership.

Mentoring

Within the narratives that were shared are examples of the way mentors served as models for our group members and made an impact on their leadership development. The theme of mentorship is more fully developed in a forthcoming chapter dedicated to the positive impact of strong mentors on feminist leadership development. Within our own LEAD group, the distributed leadership model created an environment for women to mentor each other, and this process was reported as having contributed to the leadership development of our members. Individuals with experience in a particular area regarding leadership would naturally step up in the moment, offering advice, further discussion, and support. While our group consisted of highly educated and sophisticated academic women and all having much to offer, we recognized that each had individual areas of knowledge and strength as well as gaps or dilemmas to work through. Because of our environment of collaboration, each of us, at any given time, might become a mentor to others within our group or might benefit from the mentorship of others within the group. Because of the culture of trust that we had developed, we shared willingness to be vulnerable with each other. The same individual who had previously assumed a role as mentor to others within the LEAD group might, at another time, under other circumstances, become the recipient of mentoring, gracefully slipping into the temporary role of apprentice. In essence, our group LEAD members were engaging in relational mentoring.

Conclusion

The identified themes were embedded in the narratives and in our ongoing work together as a group. Within this book, the identified themes will be more fully developed in the subsequent chapters. Each woman has expressed the ways that understanding of feminist leadership praxis has evolved. We learned to expand our definitions of leadership. We experienced the ways in which interactions with others enabled us to establish and use our voices to re-envision self and construct a leadership identity. As a group, we learned to define leadership as a post-modern concept of many intersecting voices, questioning traditional norms of leadership. It was a process of empowerment and collaboration, including peer and self-development.

At the time of this writing, much has changed since the original retreat and heart mapping activity. We have experienced a pandemic and our university, as are other universities, has adjusted to educating students virtually. We are now re-adjusting to a gradual societal recovery.

Our country is engaged in a historical racial and social awakening. The impact of recognizing issues of Diversity, Equity, Inclusion and Social Justice has impacted students in university settings and has jarred each of us to use our power to more effectively confront societal inequities and become outspoken and fearless allies to students and colleagues who are marginalized.

Members of LEAD continue to grapple with the need to be timely, inclusive, and important enough to attract women who look different than we do, who have experienced life in ways that differ from our own, and whose voices may interact with ours as we continue on our pathway of self and group leadership identity building.

References

Brown, B. (2012). *Daring greatly: How the courage to be vulnerable transforms the way we live, love, parent, and lead*. Avery.

Clinchy, B. M., Tarule, J. M., Belenky, M. F., & Goldberger, N. R. (1996). *Women's ways of knowing*. Basic Books.

Heard, G. (1999). *Heart mapping activity instructions*. https://www.wsra.org/assets/Convention/Handouts_2013/a6%20georgia%20heard%20heart%20mapping.pdf

Mouton, N. (2019). A literary perspective on the limits of leadership: Tolstoy's critique of the great man theory. *Leadership, 15*(1), 81–102. https://doi.org/10.1177/1742715017738823

O'Brien, W., Hanlon, C., & Apostolopoulos, A. (2023). Women as leaders in male-dominated sectors: A bifocal analysis of gendered organizational practices. *Gender, Work & Organization, 30*(6). https://doi.org/10.1111/gwao.13019

Seltzer, R. (2015). *The coach's guide for women professors who want a successful career and a well-balanced life*. Stylus.

3 Blocking Women's Path

Structural Barriers to Positions of Senior Leadership

Robin L. Roth

Women faculty know there is very limited opportunity for them to move into senior positions of academic leadership. Women faculty of color, a disproportionately very small group within women faculty, know they have even less chance. Simple optics and women's lived experiences within their institutions make this abundantly clear.

Demographics across institutions clearly reveal the national picture: Women in higher education are woefully underrepresented in senior positions of leadership. This reality exists in stark contrast to the steadily increased presence of women in all levels of higher education since the 1970s, both as students and employees. Women now earn more than half of all post-secondary degrees in the United States including 53% of all doctorates (computed from NCES, 2020b raw numbers). Despite their gains in Ph.D. attainment, women comprise only 47% of all full-time faculty[1] (NCES, 2020a), and as compared to full time male faculty, they are disproportionately in lower ranks, part-time and non-tenure track positions, and lesser status schools. Their presence in positions of leadership has not increased commensurately with their presence in higher education. Senior leadership continues to be extremely marginal for women across all racial/ethnic groups. This lack of progress into academic leadership positions continues in the face of legislation of the past 60 years to prohibit employment discrimination and promote increased equality and diversity in higher education.

Why are there not more women in senior positions of leadership in higher education? It would seem that as women have attained significantly more doctorates and entered the professorate in higher numbers, their ascension to senior positions should increasingly occur. So why don't we see more women at the top? And why are women of color so dramatically less proportionately represented than White women? This chapter attempts to answer these questions in terms of the structural patterns and organizational arrangements prevalent in US colleges and universities.

Understanding why there has been little change in higher ed leadership is complex. The reasons focused on in this chapter can be sorted into two major structural categories of causes within higher ed itself: (1) demographic changes

DOI: 10.4324/9781003057208-3

in higher education including the numbers of women faculty who enter higher ed, and their initial placement in rank, promotions, and retention; (2) structural factors deriving from the organizational arrangements of higher education institutions and how they do business.

Moving From Faculty to Senior Leadership

I started my own academic career as an entry-level full-time faculty hire and followed a reasonably progressive path to full professor. I didn't aspire to be an administrator, but after some years in my faculty position, and having moved up through a few rungs of the higher ed faculty ranks, like many faculty who become administrators I was spontaneously asked to fill an unanticipated open administrative role. After that initial interim position, over time I moved into other administrative roles, and sometimes back to faculty in-between or concurrently. I became a now-and-then department chair and then a director of women's studies, not unusual academic patterns for a woman, that is, mid-level administrative service without a great deal of power. But unlike most women faculty who have spells in mid-level administration, I continued on the administrative path – formally switching full-time over to "the other side" – eventually to become dean of my undergraduate college.

My relatively smooth path into increasingly higher positions of administration had its considerable challenges, but it was a unilinear, upward trajectory of increasingly higher positions. I did not encounter derailing organizational barriers and blocks to movement as so many women do, but my career from initial faculty entry to college dean was at two women's colleges, institutions where women faculty are relatively over-represented and often have more opportunity for advancement. As a professional woman, however, while I did not encounter many of the gender-based organizational blocks academic women typically experience, I did not escape the inevitable female challenges – sometimes choking – that came along with gendered family care and presented challenges to my juggle of family and work lives my male colleagues did not as frequently and severely experience.

My relatively smooth upward administrative path was further atypical in that I moved up through the administrative hierarchy with strong professional sponsorship, actively at first by my female deans and then critically by my female university president. I had women sponsors and mentors and significant academic support both inside my institution and outside of it as well.

Very formatively, I had an early career year-long sabbatical fellowship as a Mellon Scholar with legendary Peggy McIntosh at the Center on Research on Women (CRW) at Wellesley College. This was in the early years of Peggy's Mellon-funded fellowships which were to be a persistent national force in transforming college and PreK – 12 curriculum (the latter through the long-term National SEED Project). My CRW Mellon Fellowship morphed into a ten-year long continuation seminar of feminist faculty/women's studies administrators. This group provided enormous ongoing professional support which was underwritten in its first few years by funding arranged fortuitously by Peggy McIntosh, the godmother of so many feminist scholars and educational administrators. I moved institutionally from my initial position at a women's college to a faculty line in another women's college, this one within a larger university headed by another woman president. In time, she solicited and sponsored me to pick up some mid-level administrative positions and then to move to full-time middle management. She provided continued sponsorship, including nominating and providing me with institutional funding to attend the HERS year-long Women's Leadership Institute, typically a launching pad for moving a culturally diverse group of academic women into careers in senior higher education administration. My year at HERS provided a critical formal foundation in leadership with focused workshops, counseling, and training in concrete areas of senior management work (e.g., legal and policy issues, finance, personnel, job interviewing, conflict resolution, networking). I had sponsorship, mentorship, support, and a strong national network of female administrators, as well as development of essential skills and knowledge from HERS. All of these provided a strong foundation for my success as dean of a college. But as a woman moving to a senior position, my personal path upward was facilitated by invisible privileges compared to most women of color in that I had racial privilege as white, and likely invisibly amplified further by my status as middle class, native born, cisgender, heterosexual, and able-bodied.

My focus in this chapter on the structural barriers to women's advancement to senior levels of authority and power is grounded in a critical and intersectional perspective, interrogating the differential experiences of women of different race and ethnic identities in the higher ed hierarchy. But before moving to uncover and analyze the institutional barriers and whom they affect and to what degree, it is important to have a basic demographic picture of what positions women occupy in faculty and leadership, including a necessary breakdown of women by race and ethnicity in these positions. Demographic clarity is essential to provide a starting picture of missing women, stalled women, and no-longer-present women. It is a necessary structural grounding to help reveal the shared and different blocks faculty women experience due to their different positions of privilege and oppression especially based on race and ethnicity.

The most frequent path to senior leadership for all academic women is through the senior faculty ranks. Thus, any analysis of the missing women at the top needs to investigate what happens with higher education's 47% of full-time faculty who are women (NCES, 2021). After initial hire, which for full time faculty is typically as assistant professor, how do women move up through the ranks, the critical academy's hierarchical pre-stages to potential leadership? What impedes or slows down their movement up? What are the barriers within the structure and organization of higher education that make that movement harder, slower, or impossible? What is the breakdown by race and ethnicity at different ranks? Here, it is critical to utilize a consistent intersectional lens to discern and be sensitive to differential experiences of women of oppressed and privileged groups, to interrogate how intersecting identities may lead to different experiences and blocks for women of privileged and oppressed groups in higher education. But first, it's essential to uncover how many women overall are in leadership, who they are in terms of race/ethnicity, and how that corresponds to faculty demographics and movement. The answers to these questions must start with an understanding of the lay of the land: a clear demographic picture of women faculty and leaders. Then, we may analyze the structural arrangements of colleges and universities that impede or facilitate some women's movement.

Where Are the Women? Who Are the Women?

Starting at the Top: Senior Leader Demographics

Clearly, there are women in senior leadership positions in higher education. How many? How much has that changed in recent decades? Are women of color proportionately represented? At the outset, before we can get to answering those questions, we encounter a counting problem with federally reported statistics on U.S. faculty demographics with respect to race/ethnicity breakdowns. The U.S. National Center for Education Statistics (NCES) is a division within the Federal Department of Education that annually reports a huge breadth of U.S. educational trends, occupations, and data, but it does not provide a sufficiently clear annual demographic picture of women in higher education leadership. It provides less attention to higher education faculty and administrators than to elementary and secondary education data. Their available data on higher education leadership positions generally focuses somewhat narrowly on college and university presidents, but some reports include limited data on other senior academic officers such as CAOs and provosts or other leaders just below that level. That is helpful, but much of their higher education employment data has blindness to race, ethnic, and gender categories. For more accurate trend data on racial/ethnic, and other demographic indicators on higher education senior leaders by gender, especially with respect to faculty, we generally turn to additional data collected at various times and for varying purposes by non-governmental organizations such as American Association of University Professors (AAUP) and the American Council on Education's (ACE's) recent annual and occasional reports and updates on women in higher education. The Colorado Women's College 2013 study is another reliable report that can be read along with regularly shared ACE and AAUP data to build a slim demographic picture of women's leadership.

Problematic, however, is that a good portion of this data on academic women reports on women as one homogeneous category: "women." Few consistent sources provide breakdowns by race, ethnicity or any other salient social identity categories. A few of the sources have some of their data broken down by gender, other sources have some data broken down by race. But very few provide demographic data on leaders with breakdowns of gender *by race/ethnicity*. The consistent lack of attentiveness to race/ethnicity and gender simultaneously is a continuation of a historic governmental data gathering lack of understanding of the importance of the intersecting identities that so dramatically and meaningfully impact the trajectory of women's work lives. That the professional and public data collection continues this bias in the 21st century continues to be a grave omission, and it continues a historical blurring of the presence and experience of women of color.[2]

Given this basic omission of race/ethnicity breakdown in the gender data, what do we know of the incidence of women as senior academic leaders, which is mostly limited to aggregative gender data? As noted earlier, demographic reporting is sporadic on the top tier positions. Most basically, we know that women as one composite group today comprise 30% of all college presidents. That percentage doubled from 1986 to 2016, but it has remained relatively stagnant since then (ACE, 2020). There is, however, a disproportionately large difference in the breakdown of women presidents by specific self-identified racial/ethnic identity. ACE reported in 2020 that 83% of women college presidents identified as White; 7.7% as African American; 5.6% as Hispanic; and 1.2% as Asian[3] (ACE, 2020). While 17% of *all* college presidents – men and women combined – are from racial/ethnic minorities, the presidents of color (again, men and women combined) disproportionately head colleges and universities of lesser status. For example, 36% of all presidents of color are leaders of two-year institutions (ACE, 2017). It seems safe to assume that women of color presidents are a small subgroup of that 36%.

The most frequently reported job women hold prior to becoming president is as a chief academic officer (CAO) or provost (often these two titles are held jointly). In its 2016 data collected on women presidents, ACE reported that 46% of women presidents had come to their presidency directly from a CAO/provost position. The second most frequent previous job for current women presidents was being a president; that is, moving from one presidential job to another. Only 14% of women reported being hired as president from a job outside higher education (ACE, 2020). Thus, CAO/provost position is crucial for becoming a president for women: It typically precedes a first presidency for women, and a first presidency often leads to another presidency.

Demonstrating the narrowing of the ladder up for women of color, in 2009 only 3% of CAOs/provosts were women of color (ACE, 2017). In terms of administrative jobs just below CAOs, there are few if any available large-scale reports that include race/ethnic breakdowns for women. Using figures on all women due to lack of race/ethnic breakdown, the AAUP reported that in 2011 50% of the "central administrative officers" (associate provost, dean of faculty, but also including other non-academic line administrators such as dean of students) and 36% of deans were women (AAUP, 2011). We can see the disproportionately low number of women in positions that might lead up to CAO or higher, but not what the place of women of color is in those ranks, at least not by the reliable, regular reporters of this data.

The term "pipeline" is often used to refer to movement of women up the academic ladder from faculty to senior leaders. It's a misleading term, implying an upward flow for women. The statistical picture of top positions provided here demonstrates that the higher we go, the fewer women proportionately there are. Demographic presence of women in top positions indicates that the so-called pipeline is considerably narrow and with impediments for White women, but for women of color it is at best a trickle. It seems appropriate to conclude, as Kellerman and Rhode do, that for so many women, and certainly for women of color, "the pipeline has been a pipe dream" (2014, p. 24).

"Glass ceiling" is another obfuscating popularly used term in higher education hierarchies, as in organizations in general. It describes a purported invisible barrier to top occupational positions for women and people of color. The metaphor implies that aspirants from oppressed groups may be blocked to leadership positions by this transparent barrier which they must crash through, the metaphor including a sense that this crashing through is possible by the "best and brightest." A clever metaphor for organizational status quo in that it leaves it to the power of the women and folks of color to break that barrier – if they can in organizations which are structured in visible and invisible patterns that impede their progress up.

Recently, some critical writers have described these restrictive leadership layers as more like *gated communities* rather than as impeded by penetrable class ceilings in that they more accurately rely on the willingness of privileged class leaders to open up their "gated" top occupational tier to an individual of a typically blocked gender or racial group. That is, the gated community concept describes the necessity of the dominant essentially homogeneous elite leadership group, who typically engage in restricted, biased assessment and judgment to, in very limited cases, *allow in* a very selective individual from social groups who are usually excluded from leadership. In her excellent volume co-edited with Johanna Maes, *Journeys of Social Justice: Women of Color Presidents in the Academy,* Menah Pratt-Clarke proposes to replace the glass ceiling metaphor with "plantation roof" as a more apt term for African American women, placing the senior-level blockage they experience "within the complex construct of enslavement, in which African American women were subject to experiences of oppression, denigration, dehumanization, marginalization, racism, and sexism from White men, White women, and even Black men" (Pratt-Clarke & Maes, 2017, p. 13). Gabriella Guttiérrez y Muhs (2017) refers to the "adobe ceiling" for Latinas based on historical patterns of exclusion, while other authors of color suggest similar race and ethnically based terms to describe the interlocking oppressions experienced by faculty women of color in other groups that almost entirely close them out of leadership. These authors' illuminative assessments of the barriers to leadership join a growing body of rich narrative accounts by women of color that present the strengths and strategies they use to support themselves as they aspire to and actually do move into leadership in the academy (see, e.g., Baldwin & Griffin, 2015; Guttierrez y Muhs et al., 2012; Pratt-Clarke & Maes, 2017).

Movement Up the Academic Hierarchy: Faculty Demographics

As noted earlier, the most typical path to senior academic leadership for women starts from a faculty line and proceeds upward through faculty ranks to higher levels of administrative leadership. Tracing backward then, from demographics on senior administrative women, we need to look below to the dispersion of women faculty through the hierarchy of faculty ranks to understand the potential pool of senior administrators, and then to see how and when women of differing race/ethnic groups – move up the faculty hierarchy. The NCES annually reports on a wide range of educational indicators and measures, including data on college and university faculty. Its data on faculty is robust, with annual raw numbers, and their practice for many years is to provide breakdowns of faculty by the very broad categories of race and ethnicity used by the federal government (currently Black, Asian and Pacific Islander, Hispanic, Native and Indigenous People).

Current NCES data on faculty demonstrates that women, as an aggregate category, hold 47% of all full-time faculty positions, with men holding the remaining 53%. Using the federal racial census categories and the raw numbers provided by the NCES, we can compute the racial/ethnic group breakdown of women faculty in descending order of presence: White women 69%; Asian/Pacific Islander women 10.2%; Black women 7.4%; Hispanic women 5.8%; Two + races 1.2%; American Indian/Alaska Native 5%; the remaining women faculty are reported as non-citizens or unknown race (my percentages computed based on NCES, 2019, Table 315.20). This racial breakdown of the 47% of faculty who are women provides somber clarity of today's numbers of women of color among all women faculty. It is disappointing that the NCES does not regularly present the percentages so that there could be a simple and publicly visible and yearly updated clear picture of female faculty in terms of the critically important racial/ethnic breakdowns of all full-time faculty women.

What about the dispersion of women into faculty jobs and especially into the hierarchy of faculty ranks? Women workers are generally vertically segregated in the academic labor market, as in the US labor market overall. That is, they are clustered disproportionately into lower ranks of jobs within job sectors, with unequal access to moving upward to higher level positions in their fields. Accordingly, women faculty are disproportionately clustered into part-time, non-tenure track, and lower faculty ranks in the university, occupying those lower status realms much more so than do men. Despite aspiring to higher status positions, many of these women are never able to break out of these lower levels. This is especially true in the part-time or adjunct realm. Higher education relies to an extraordinary extent on a contingent, part-time labor force for its faculty with 46% of all faculty nation-wide in part-time/adjunct positions in 2018 (NCES, 2020a). The percentage has been consistently growing in the 21st century, but recent challenges in higher education, including declining enrollments, leave it uncertain if the part-time increase will continue to grow. There are predictable gender differences in this contingent labor force with 50% of all women faculty in part-time positions in 2018 versus only 43% of male faculty similarly part-time. (NCES, 2020a).

Women's vertical occupational segregation can be seen as well in their disproportionate occupation of non-tenure track lines, usually dead-end faculty positions, that is, providing no opportunity to movement to tenure or promotions which leads as well to less job security than tenure track and tenured positions. This is another structural factor that contributes to their experiencing a diminished ability to move into leadership. In 2018 women held 50% of all tenure *track* positions, but just 39% of women faculty were actually tenured. Breaking tenure track down by race/ethnicity, we find women of color much more rarely on that path than White women, with Asian women holding 5.3% of women's tenure track lines; Black women holding 3.8%, and Latinas holding 3.1%. That can be compared as well to the disproportionately low percentage of women of color who are actually tenured: out of the only 39% of tenured faculty who are women, just 3.5% are Asian; 2.3% are Black, 2.6% are Latina (*Catalyst*, 2020). These numbers make clear the much more sequestered and narrowed opportunities for tenure, as well as for full-time work that women of color have compared to White women – and White women, more privileged, still with much less opportunity to enjoy the security and privileges of tenure than men in general.

Simultaneous with their disproportionate experience of vertical segregation in less status conferring college and university positions in the US higher ed hierarchy, women faculty may also experience horizontal occupational segregation in higher education, that is, the general occupational tendency for oppressed and privileged groups to be disproportionately clustered across the horizon of fields in the labor force, with men and White workers more likely to be in the sectors that provide higher social status and higher pay. Women faculty are clustered more than men in higher education in office areas and disciplines that are typically less status-conferring and with lower pay, academic fields such as education, social services, student services, social sciences, thus making it harder for them to move up in rank from these less status-conferring areas and disciplines to senior academic leadership. These two forms of segregation – vertical and horizontal – may be experienced by women of all identities, but they are much more prevalent for women of color in higher education as in the occupational world at large. Simple optics demonstrates this clearly to those of us on the ground looking critically and intersectionality within and across organizations, but demographic analysis of women in higher education occupations make the case even more clear.

Looking across the hierarchy of faculty ranks makes evident the impact of vertical segregation on women as a whole group, but even more so when broken down by race and ethnicity. While this is not surprising to many women faculty, the numbers need to be collected, analyzed, reported, and highlighted more so we may bring attention and clarity to this process and to the differential and unequal faculty paths of women in general and especially of women of color.

Looking then at faculty by rank, of all the men and women who are full-time faculty, women faculty as a whole comprise 34.3% of all full professors; 46.4% of associate professors; and 52.9% of assistant professors (*Catalyst*, 2020). This demonstrates a definite skewing of women as a whole into the lower ranks. But the aggregated numbers (i.e., of *all* women) hide significant racial/ethnic disparities among women faculty. Women of color are disproportionately in lower ranks given their actual percentages in faculty as a whole (Table 3.1).

Since it is the senior ranks of associate and full professors that lead or could lead to promotion to senior administrative positions, it is important to have a clear picture of the percentage of all faculty in senior ranks along with its breakdown by race/ethnicity to understand a critical structural barrier to women moving to senior leadership. Looking at full professors, we see that only 34% of women faculty are currently full professors, an improvement over the past, but still far short of men's status. Breaking women's 2018 34% of full professors aggregate down by race/ethnicity; however, we find (rounding for simplicity) that 27% of them are White; 3% are Asian/Pacific Islander; 2% are Black and less than 1% each are Hispanic, Native American/Alaska Native, or Two + races (NCES cited in *Catalyst*, 2020).

Demonstrating further differences between women faculty that may have a bearing on differential ability to move to the top is the percentage of women faculty who are in tenure track or tenured positions. As noted earlier, in 2018 women held 50% of tenure track positions, but just 39% of women faculty were actually tenured.

Table 3.1 Percentage of faculty ranks held by women of color (*Catalyst*, 2020)

	Asian women	*Black women*	*Latina women*
Assistant Professor	5.8%	4.0%	2.9%
Associate Professor	4.8%	3.0%	2.6%
Full Professor	2.8%	1.6%	2.1%

Breaking tenure track down by race/ethnicity, we find women of color much more rarely on that path than White women, with Asian women holding 5.3% of the 50% tenure track positions held by women: Black women holding 3.8%, and Latinas holding 3.1%. This should be further compared as well to the disproportionately low percentage of women of color who are actually tenured: out of the 39% of tenured faculty who are women, just 3.5% are women of color (NCES cited in *Catalyst*, 2020).

This demographic picture of women's place in the faculty hierarchy demonstrates a marked occupational skew vertically in lower level ranks and horizontally across lower status departments and disciplines. This provides a part of the structural explanation for why we find a disproportionately fewer number of women in higher ed leadership. Obviously, the fewer the women in feeder paths and positions, the shallower the pool to move up to higher positions and then on to top leadership. Understanding the demographics of women in faculty and administration is a critical necessary step to peeling back the layers that impede women's movement to leadership. The demographics make clear the much narrower opportunities for movement experienced by all women, and more so by women of color compared to White women, due to their respective numbers in faculty ranks, and especially their thinned-out presence in the senior ranks. While all women experience horizontal segregation, that is, sequestering in the lower faculty ranks, the increasingly fewer women, and even more so, the much smaller percentage of women of color in senior faculty ranks, demonstrate how narrow the "pipeline" is for them to the top.

Moving Beyond Demographics to Other Structural Causes of Exclusion: Further Barriers

Demographics of women faculty's dispersion in the academic hierarchy provide a necessary but incomplete explanation of the missing women at the top. The numbers do count shrinking numbers of women – disproportionately – as we move to increasingly higher positions across the academic areas are a formidable barrier to more women available to move up further. Starting with demographic clarity is a necessary but not sufficient explanation of why so few women are in senior academic leadership. Understanding the basic structural layout of women does not explain enough. It doesn't explain *why* the numbers of women shrink so appreciably as we climb upward in analysis. It does not provide an explanation as to why the presence of women of color diminishes even more disproportionately than White women. To assume – or simply state – that the answer is simply "discrimination" is to fail to come to grips with the breadth, depth, and complexity of the problem. The problem can't be remedied, or even ameliorated significantly, without a thorough and clear unpacking of the vague explanation of "discrimination." Clearly, the process of blockage is more invidious, more hidden, more complex than a simple crude discriminatory passing over women for men. Overt discrimination does occur, as we all know, but there are other formative, formidable, widespread structural patterns that create an intricate and dynamic pattern keeping women – and even disproportionately more so women of color – at the margins. And many of these patterns are not recognized. Therefore, they persist and are replicated. Those are the barriers we need to turn to in order to amplify the basic demographic picture that has now been established.

Complex interwoven higher education barriers operate at both the micro level of interaction between people and small groups, and at the macro level of the actual structural arrangements and patterns of higher education. To say that there are structural blocks for faculty women's ascension to leadership is to assert that women's advancement is blunted by higher education's organizational processes and administrative features, and as well by blocks that emanate from social and cultural values, ideas, and patterns structured within the institutionalized processes and structures of the very organization of colleges and universities – and this in addition to the formidable sociocultural patterns outside the institution that are a whole other force of variables contributing barriers, such as women's disproportionate caring responsibilities outside the workplace and the lack of caring facilities, and other social and cultural factors interfering with women's ability to participate in their work lives in a way similar to most men. The social and cultural barriers are well discussed in other arenas and publications and settings, and so I will retain the focus in this chapter more exclusively on the less recognized and understood structural barriers within higher ed organizations themselves.

21st-Century Colleges and Universities and Corporatization

Institutions of higher education have instituted many formative changes since the latter decades of the 20th century in response to perceived needs for institutional stability and growth. These combined changes, sometimes referred to critically as corporatization, include increased focus on the bottom line of finances and tuition service; pressure on faculty to obtain external funding sources and large-scale grants; heightened attentiveness to competition and external markets, branding, image, and niche; and other administrative and organizational structures, many of them more typically found in the for-profit economic sector. These economic structural changes have direct impact on faculty, most notably a lesser reliance on part-time as opposed to full time faculty (the percentage split now at about 70%/30%, respectively); decrease of tenured positions; smaller workforce of administrative support workers; increased centralization of decision-making concomitant with a narrowed role of faculty governance; increased pressure on faculty to secure external funding for research; increased research demands on full-time faculty; changes in the valuation and status of some forms of research and some disciplines, especially but not only interdisciplinary departments (such as gender and ethnic studies) being seen as "less serious" or important. While many of these changes are acknowledged as having strong faculty impact, they are not gender and race neutral. Their connection to women faculty's ascension to higher level leadership needs to be investigated and with an intersectional lens.

Gendered Organizations and the Ideal Worker: What's a Woman to Do?

In an influential 1990 article in *Gender & Society,* sociologist Joan Acker introduced the term "gendered organizations" to describe the pervasive and unacknowledged patriarchal structural and operating values, patterns, and systems of large-scale organizations (Acker, 1990). While it is not surprising today to note that the patterns of privilege and oppression that are woven throughout the larger society and its social institutions find their way into the structure of large-scale organizations such as colleges and universities, Acker described contemporary large-scale organizations as not only gendered, but gendered *processes* where "both gender and sexuality have been obscured through a gender neutral, asexual discourse" (1990, p. 140). Describing higher education – or any institution – as a gendered process is to expose gendering as endemic through the institution, not merely a simple "addition to ongoing processes" (Acker, 1990). It involves language; ideology; dress; spatial and temporal layout and timing of work; job descriptions; work assignments; leadership values; opportunities for advancement; and even ways of conceptualizing the organization and its processes (Bird, 2011; Acker, 1990). In her later writings, Acker advanced the term "inequality regimes" to encompass the interlocking system of racial, class, and gender discrimination in large-scale work organizations, and the extreme genderization and racialization of top leadership positions (see, for example, Acker, 2006).

Acker further described gendered institutions as having a guiding model of an ideal worker, and that ideal worker is male. The ideal worker is one who is devoted to the organization, available to work at varying hours, relatively free of childcare or care of other family members that might interfere with work hours or responsibilities. He has a manner of dressing, speech, interacting with others (a manner we would generally identify as "male"). He has a management style that is based on the way men typically lead and manage: more directly, authoritatively, hierarchically, independently, as opposed to a management style that is more collaborative, relational, cooperative (Acker, 1990). Accordingly, women faculty are assessed and judged compared to the organizational ideal worker image, a masculinized – and racialized – model that is a poor fit for many women, and which many do not wish to necessarily embody nor employ. Women's work style – broadly interpreted – is judged for promotion, and their lack of "good fit" with the ideal worker model impacts their promotions, often in unstated or unacknowledged or under understood ways. It certainly impacts their movement into leadership.

The ideal worker and ideal leader models fit women of color even less well than White women. Women from racial and ethnic minority groups may possess work patterns judged to be more at odds with the models – masculinized ideal worker models – that are conducive to promotion and success. Often further contributing to difficulty for women of color are the racist cultural stereotypes ascribed to them by their specific presenting cultural identity, for example, the angry Black woman; the submissive, soft-spoken, gentle Asian woman; the hot-headed or spirited Latina. Racial and ethnic minority women thus have the additional burden of being judged negatively on the basis of their cultural stereotype in addition to not embodying closely enough the masculinized and racialized model of the ideal worker.

To the extent that she differs from the ideal worker model, a woman's work performance may be problematized. And if she doesn't fit the ideal worker model, she will have more limited opportunity for promotion to senior leadership. When women faculty do adopt more masculine styles (e.g., exhibiting patterns of directness, being assertive, taking charge, working independently, even literally "suiting up") they are often judged as inappropriate, or unfeminine, strident, or "too ethnic." This presents a double bind for women who often understand the importance of ideal worker model. If they adopt it, they may be judged negatively for violating sociocultural stereotypes about women's behavior; if they don't adopt it, they risk not being seen as successful and/or lacking leadership qualities.

The Continued Problem of Numbers

The demographic numbers play into the gendered organization problem for all women, and more so for women of color. Being in the statistical minority matters; it imposes many problems for women. Males' overrepresentation both in the senior faculty ranks and in leadership positions means that men disproportionately comprise the bulk of important committees and leadership roles that make recommendations and/or decisions for tenure and promotion. Male judgments and the unspoken ideal worker model flourish where women are underrepresented in these determinative roles. Thus, women's and men's imbalance in numbers in the organization has bearing on their being disproportionately in lower level and lower status positions. In her influential 1977 study *Men and Women of the Corporation,* sociologist and former *Harvard Business Review* editor Rosabeth Moss Kanter introduced the notion of "homosocial reproduction" to describe the choices men in power make – reproducing their own profiles as workers and leaders – as they recruit and promote members in the large-scale corporation she studied (Kanter, 1977/1993).

Kanter also described the impact of the low numbers on women in organizations, especially the very few in management and leadership positions, making them more visible and seemingly different by virtue of their small numbers

(Kanter, 1977/1993). Being such a very small minority among faculty, and an even smaller presence in higher leadership, women of color are more often judged, and judged negatively, based on a confluence of factors: unconscious bias, deviation from the ideal worker model, and even the seeming exoticism of their rarity when they get into positions of power. Such judgments typically create additional barriers to their further advancement.

Due to their very low numbers, women of color often experience isolation, lack of sufficient networking opportunities, and at the same time a sense of heightened visibility and scrutiny (see, e.g., essays by women of color college and university presidents in Pratt-Clarke & Maes, 2017; Guttierrez y Muhs et al., 2012; Niemann et al., 2020). White women who advance to senior levels where they are a statistical minority typically also experience these challenging work conditions and perceptions, but in a much less extreme fashion due to their numbers providing a degree of support, networking, and colleagueship that women of color do not possess. Add to this that White women do not encounter racist stereotypes on top of gendered stereotypes and otherness that flow from the ideal worker model.

Tenure and Promotion Barriers

The increasingly smaller percentage of women as we look up the hierarchy of faculty ranks is in itself a structural barrier to equity in tenure and promotion. As presented earlier, it is a national demographic reality that men comprise the majority of senior faculty eligible for serving on Rank, Promotion, and Tenure committees, but one of several structural features that have dynamic involvement in faculty women's barriers to upward movement. Faculty who serve on promotion and tenure committees are almost always by institutional policy associate and senior professors. Currently, 55% of associates and 65% of full professors are male (Flaherty, 2020) which in itself makes the demographic pool for committee membership male dominated by numbers alone, let alone other factors that might increase male membership on these committees. Beyond just the numbers-composition problem, the committees and administrators involved in tenure and promotion recommendations and decisions do so in terms of covert and overt models of successful faculty performance. These models are based on the ideal worker, homosocial reproduction, shared patriarchal definitions of successful faculty performance, as well as unconscious bias.

Across the United States the most frequent primary criterion for tenure and promotion is faculty research. Yet, women faculty spend less time in research and more time in service and teaching than their male colleagues (Bird, 2011). For some women, tilting their balance more toward service and teaching is by their own choice; for some it is due to the needs of their departments and the university, as expressed by deans and supervisors.

Making the research primacy more problematic for women is that not all research is deemed of equal value for tenure and promotion. Certain forms of research (e.g., qualitative) and certain disciplines (e.g., business and finance; many science fields) are seen as less important, while fields and research that are more heavily populated by males are often judged as more important or weightier. Notable numbers of faculty of color as well as White women engage in research methods and in interdisciplinary fields (e.g., qualitative research; gender and ethnic studies; multicultural and diversity fields) that are often judged as "lighter" in academia. This bias in judging faculty scholarship and work adds to other structural burdens women and people of color encounter in their tenure and promotion processes.

While teaching may not be the primary criterion for tenure and promotion of faculty nation-wide, it is at the least an important component among several other components, some of which have inherent biases further hindering women faculty and even more so women of color faculty. One frequently discussed problem area, with even more danger for women of color compared to their also impacted White women peers, is in the use of student evaluations in promotion and tenure decisions. Often, to the detriment of women and faculty of color, student evaluation may be given serious consideration when they are negative. Much research exists that demonstrates that women and faculty of color are more negatively evaluated by students and that students make more complaints to administrators about women and faculty of color. But there are many factors that may impact student evaluations beyond singular faculty variables of gender or other faculty identity statuses, and recent studies demonstrate the need for more complex study and analysis to have stronger basis for developing and instituting changes (e.g., see Chavez & Mitchell, 2019).

The Institutional Service Burden

The structural changes in higher education over the past several decades can lead to problems for all faculty. Cross-national hiring practices that have shifted the majority of faculty hires from full-time to part-time have had a significant impact on full-time faculty work life especially due to their multifaceted roles in colleges and universities. As universities and colleges hire higher percentages of contingent and part-time workers, including among faculty ranks, faculty have necessarily taken on heavier service loads. This includes an increased burden on smaller pools of full-time faculty to provide necessary and important service in cross-campus committee work, curriculum development and oversight, student recruitment and retention activities, secretarial/administrative tasks, and other organizational operations. Women faculty experience this changing burden, on average, even more than their male counterparts, as higher education relies on women more than men to perform much other informal services due to other structural issues such as reduced administrative support staff; providing supports for female students and students of color; supporting more formal and informal advising of students, especially women and those of racial/ethnic groups; under acknowledged support to other workers (support staff and other non-faculty workers). This informal support, mentoring, and care work is a significant part of faculty women's work life and work time, and it is a by-product of many of the increasingly corporate structural features of higher education. Their higher share of caring, support, advising, mentoring work, much of it informal and not recognized, contributes to their work life and work burden, and it is not easily or usually acknowledged as a contribution when women faculty are assessed regarding job performance and for promotion and tenure.

Since faculty service in universities falls almost exclusively to full-time faculty who in 2021 comprised only 56% of total faculty (NCES, 2021), this needs to be understood as putting a disproportionately larger burden on full-time women faculty than on men due to women's smaller numbers. This leads, at least in part, to women faculty being asked to serve on more committees than men (Bird, 2011). Again, for the population of women of color, the demographics are even more burdensome than for White women. Women faculty are asked by supervisors, colleagues, and their deans to provide more service out of an institutional desire for "balance," or at least representation, on committees and in other activities. As women, and especially disproportionately women of color, experience being asked "for diversity needs" to join committees, they do so, burdening themselves with service loads that are generally much heavier than those of men (Bird, 2011). Yet, much service work is narrowly visible, even when it is requested of women by their superiors and/or colleagues. This makes it less valued in assessments and promotions. When it is presented in a formal report of a woman's work life (e.g., in a tenure or promotion application), it is not valued as much as scholarship and teaching. In fact, in my own experience as a dean, a chair, a rank and promotion committee member, and a faculty union chief steward, I often heard a women's heavy service contributions judged negatively, as evidence of a woman having "the wrong commitments" – wrong, that is, as opposed her doing more scholarship.

In a recent analysis of a large national database of faculty, coupled with an analysis of faculty annual reports at two large public universities, Guarino and Borden (2017) found that women faculty provided approximately 25% more service than males, when controlling for differences in rank, department or discipline, race, and ethnicity. They found many complexities in the differences, with variations in different disciplines and departments, gender of chair, size of department, even faculty rank (e.g., associate women had larger service commitments than did assistant and full professors).

Karen Pyke addressed the often-asked question of "why don't women faculty just say no?" But women faculty acknowledge they don't have true freedom to deny many such requests as they may be subsequently judged negatively for turndowns in their own tenure and promotion processes. It is so important to counter this "why don't they just say no" question with an understanding that the question itself passes the responsibility for service overload to the overloaded women which Pyke aptly points out, "exacerbates gender-blind sexism in academia" (Pyke, 2015, p. 89). It is important to acknowledge and understand that the overload of service is not just done by women who find themselves in an institutional environment where declining such requests has dangers for them; women frequently report they take on an overload of service burdens because want to help other women – who they recognize are caught in a biased system – so those asked often "say yes" and participate in committees that pass judgment or policy on work and life issues that affect women greatly.

A recent article in *Inside Higher Education* with the apt title of "Promoting Gender Equity or Sexism?" provided a provocative example of an institutionally well-intentioned yet burdensome service policy for faculty. The author described a new University of Glasgow policy requiring all doctoral defenses by women students to be judged by a committee with at least one woman faculty member (Grove, 2018). In a desire to "balance out" defenses, Glasgow's senior women faculty are formally asked by university policy to "protect and support" female students – once again, putting the burden on women to ameliorate recognized gender discrimination against women doctoral students. This Glasgow example can be seen in the context of other committees where women, and university administration itself, feel a need to protect oppressed individuals with an inequitable and recognized gender burden. Will ensuring one faculty woman on a defense provide "representation," and thereby equity? How is one female faculty member at a defense providing true equity for female doctoral defendants? I can say from sometimes having been that one White committee woman, that one female can have a formidable uphill task in this regard. And what of the burden for the women who are called upon to provide "the balance" in so many committees, especially given their smaller numbers among faculty compared to men? Is this to be the "fix" for committees that are thought to have compositional biases and discriminatory practices? Is the "protective" woman committee member unscathed in such roles?

Given their disproportionately small numbers, women of color report feeling especially compelled to join committees that make important decisions affecting other people of color and women. Narratives by senior women of color administrators are replete with experiencing the double bind of compelling needs to protect and support the advancement of women of color in higher ed by disproportionate committee service and other volunteering, with reported crushing impact on their workload (see, e.g., Pratt-Clarke, 2017 and essays in Pratt-Clarke & Maes, 2017, among a growing body of narratives).

Women of color are also relatively more burdened by the informal female load of institutional care work due to the dearth of women faculty and administrators and the increased numbers of students and other workers of color who need informal support and advising and turn to faculty women of color. The lack of support for people of color, coupled with a more difficult institutional racial environment for students and employees from oppressed groups, leads them to turn especially to faculty women of color for support in institutions that recruit them but do not adequately support them, as well as the racial and other difficult-related issues they encounter in higher education. Again, the narrative accounts in published studies provide a large and compelling body of examples of the demands on and the service of women of color in this fashion, service that is seriously underrecognized and unrewarded. Further, this burden takes time and resources away from their own teaching and research, as well as from their personal, out-of-work lives, overall experienced as an enormous commitment of time and resources for women of color. (e.g., see discussions in this burgeoning and compelling body of literature by women in Baldwin & Griffin, 2015; Guttierrez y Muhs et al., 2012; Niemann et al., 2020; Pratt-Clarke & Maes, 2017).

Amado Padillo proffers the term *cultural taxation* to refer to this overload of time in service that faculty of color contribute to the university. He describes the institutionally necessary individual "requests" to participate in a relatively high level of service activities to compensate for the low numbers of faculty of color (Padillo, 1994). Padillo reports faculty of color are disproportionately on committees of diversity and equity, mentoring junior faculty of color, attending recruitment and retention activities, serving on standing committees. In essence, they are spreading themselves across the institution to provide representation and visibility as well in necessary and important activities outside the classroom and their own professional and research projects. Beyond such formal service obligations, women faculty of color report their much higher levels of informal and formal advising of students – students of color, that is – as well as informal support and advising of staff of color. June Williams describes how women faculty of color are often called upon to be a "one person minority affairs office" (Williams, 2015 as cited in Pratt-Clarke & Maes, 2017) in their burdensome engagement in time-intensive informal, uncompensated, and often non-recognized invisible labor, which includes essential mentoring, supporting, advocating, and even "mothering" academic workers and students out of duty as well as in response to administrative asks. This cultural tax – whether voluntary or not – detracts from the more institutionally valued activities that are counted more for faculty promotion and advancement.

The tenure and promotion processes in general are not gender neutral, even if there is a woman or women on the committee (as the University of Glasgow policy dictates). Women's family roles are widely accepted to present more difficulty to them than to their male colleagues with respect to the need for heavy research on top of their teaching and service responsibilities. With respect to tenure and promotion, women in tenure tracks or in lower faculty ranks often find themselves in the crux of conflict between simultaneous timing of their potential pregnancies/childbearing years and the university-imposed tenure clock or promotion to senior ranks. This has been acknowledged by many universities in the past

20 years by the process of "stopping the clock" for such women – should they request it. Women often express fear of using this option when it is available. They are concerned that invoking a time off the clock will be judged negatively in their subsequent evaluation for promotion or tenure. Stopping the clock is at best a very modest and limited accommodation that does not consider the several years of childbearing and family care that falls so disproportionately on women.

Care Work and Service

Higher Education has a need for much informal service due the structural changes mentioned earlier such as reductions in full-time faculty, administrative and support staff and other employees as well as women and People of color experiencing covert and overt discrimination in the institution or other gender and racial difficulties, among other needs.

This informal support, which is provided by mentoring and other care work, is a significant part of faculty women's work life and work time, and it is a by-product of many of the increasingly corporate structural features of higher education. Women's higher share of caring, support, advising, and mentoring work contributes to their work life and work burden, and it is not easily or usually acknowledged as a contribution when women faculty are assessed regarding job performance and for their tenure and promotion.

Women of color are relatively more burdened by the female load of care work due to the dearth of faculty and administrators of color and the increased numbers of Students and other workers of color who often are informally supported and advised by faculty women of color. The lack of supports and more difficult work conditions for students and employees of color lead them to turn to the faculty of color for support in institutions that recruit them, but do not adequately support them and the racial and other related issues they encounter both within and outside of higher education. Once again, the narrative accounts in published studies provide a formidable body of examples of the need and service of women of color in this fashion, service that is formally unrecognized and unrewarded. Further, it takes time and resources away from their own teaching and research, as well as from their personal, out-of-work lives. Soma Sen provides the huge cost of the service burden: "As women faculty of color, occupying multiple marginalized spaces, we often face "cultural taxation which has been recognized as a stealth killer of an academic" (Sen, 2020; see also Baldwin & Griffin, 2015; Guttierrez y Muhs et al., 2012; Niemann et al., 2020; Pratt-Clarke & Maes, 2017; Whitaker & Grollman, 2018).

Contradictory Narratives of Diversity, Equity, and Inclusion

The gendered and racialized structure of colleges and universities flies in the face of contemporary discourse in universities, even contradicting some institutions' mission statements and strategic plans that speak of themselves as egalitarian or meritocratic, or working toward that. The impact of these institutional narratives is formidable in the gendering and racializing of higher education institutions. As Ely and Meyerson (2000) explain, "These narratives [of gender and race blindness] are so powerful – people just "know" them to be true . . . [they] construct and sustain all aspects of organizational 'reality'" (pp. 116–117). These forces are a combined powerful tool against recognition of structural bias against women and people of color and ultimately against change. These narratives currently succeed in blurring and concealing the very structure of contemporary colleges and blunting the progress of women professors who wish to move into positions of middle and senior leadership. Movement of aspiring women faculty to equity in promotion in rank and to senior leadership can only contribute to making colleges and universities the equitable institutions of higher learning they claim to want to be.

Notes

1 As noted here, 47% (rounded off) of US full-time faculty are women. The remaining women faculty are contingent (sometimes referred to as part-time or adjunct). In this chapter, I will usually be talking about full-time women faculty as those are the women faculty who are most likely to be candidates for senior administrative positions. But other writers may not make clear qualification or distinction, or from the morass of differing data points (which I discuss later in the chapter), there is a bit of confusion or ambiguity or incomplete reporting. In other chapters of this volume, the authors may be referring to all women faculty without qualification to part-time or full-time. But in this chapter, the distinction is very important to make due to the very differing circumstances of work life and the focus of this chapter on women's blockage from moving to senior positions, a path mostly available to some full-time faculty, but very rarely to contingent faculty who are in much lower status job category and with less qualifying experience due to their usually narrowly defined teaching roles.

2 The lack of regular breakdowns of gender by race and ethnicity in large national databases is an egregious problem. By reporting mainly aggregative data on all women lumped together, we are not able to see the differential patterns of women in different racial and ethnic groups. At times in my analysis, I had to use data from different studies and databases to piece together some outlines of the different picture for women of varied race/ethnic groups. The most available and relied upon regular data is by NCES, but they and even the major NGO sources fail to provide regular and consistent breakdowns by gender and race/ethnicity as I note above. Sadly, even the well-regarded and cited Colorado Women's Study (2013) has only one data table out of 19 that provides breakdowns of women academics by race/ethnicity. Bottom line: the research and literature on women in leadership in higher education is still hampered by the same focus: public data collection on women as though all are white, and any focus on race and ethnicity is as though all the people of color are men – or that these identities are not meaningful enough to report and connect. The overall incomplete and crude data reporting reminded me of the brilliant title of the 1982 feminist classic:*All the Women Are White, All the Blacks Are Men, But Some of Us Are Brave* (Hull et al., 1982/1993): the racial analysis ignores

gender, the gender analysis ignores race. It is unchanged since Hull, Bell-Scott, and Smith so cogently raised this problem more than 40 years ago.

3 As noted here, 47% (rounded off) of US full-time faculty are women. The remaining women faculty are contingent (sometimes referred to as part-time or adjunct). In this chapter, I will usually be talking about full-time women faculty as those are the women faculty who are most likely to be candidates for senior administrative positions. But other writers may not make clear qualification or distinction, or from the morass of differing data points (which I discuss later in the chapter), there is a bit of confusion or ambiguity or incomplete reporting. In other chapters of this volume, the authors may be referring to all women faculty without qualification to part-time or full-time. But in this chapter the distinction is very important to make due to the very differing circumstances of work life and the focus of this chapter on women's blockage from moving to senior positions, a path mostly available to some full-time faculty, but very rarely to contingent faculty who are in much lower status job category and with less qualifying experience due to their usually narrowly defined teaching roles.

References

Acker, J. (1990). Hierarchies, jobs, bodies: A theory of gendered organizations. *Gender & Society*, *4*, 139–158.

Acker, J. (2006). Inequality regimes: Gender, class, and race in organizations. *Gender and Society*, *20*(4), 441–464. http://www.jstor.org/stable/27640904

American Association of University Professors (AAUP). (2011). Washington, DC. https://www.aaup.org/article/2011-bulletin-aaup

American Council on Education (ACE). (2017). *Minority presidents profile*. https://www.aceacps.org/minority-presidents/.

American Council on Education (ACE). (2020). *Moving the needle: Advancing women in higher education leadership*. https://www.acenet.edu/Programs-Services/Pages/communities/Moving-the-Needle.aspx

Baldwin, C. P., & Griffin, M. D. (2015). Challenges of race and gender for Black women in the academy. In K. De Welde & A. Stepnick (Eds.), *Disrupting the culture of silence: Confronting gender inequality and making change in higher education* (pp. 55–66). Stylus.

Bird, S. R. (2011). Unsettling universities' incongruous, gendered bureaucratic structures: A case-study approach. *Gender, Work and Organization*, (2), 202–230. https://search.ebscohost.com/login.aspx?direct=true&db=edsgao&AN=edsgcl.249618444&site=eds-live&scope=site

Catalyst. (2020). *Quick takes: Women in the US.* https://www.catalyst.org/research/women-in-academia/

Chavez, K., & Mitchell, C. V. (2019). Exploring bias in student evaluations: Gender, race, and ethnicity. *Political Science & Politics*, *53*(2), 270–274. https://doi.org/10.1017/S1049096519001744

Colorado Women's Study. (2013). *Benchmarking women's leadership in the United States*. Colorado Women's College, University of Denver.

Ely, R. J., & Meyerson, D. E. (2000). Theories of gender in organizations: A new approach to organizational analysis and change. *Research in Organizational Behavior*, *22*, 103–151.

Flaherty, C. (2020, December 10). New analysis of faculty, pay, representation. *Inside Higher Ed*. https://www.insidehighered.com/quicktakes/2020/12/10/new-analysis-faculty-pay-representation

Grove. (2018, October 18). Promoting gender equity or sexism? *Inside Higher Education.com*. https://www.insidehighered.com/news/2018/10/18/university-glasgow-requires-doctoral-defense-panels-female-phd-candidates-have-least
Guarino, C. M., & Borden, V. M. H. (2017). Faculty service loads and gender: Are women taking care of the academic family? *Research in Higher Education*, *58*, 672–694. https://doi.org/10.1007/s11162-017-9454-2
Guttierrez y Muhs, G. (2017). The adobe ceiling over the yellow brick road. In M. Pratt-Clarke & M. Maes (Eds.), *Journeys of social justice: Women of color presidents in the academy* (pp. 31–45). Peter Lang.
Guttierrez y Muhs, G., Niemann, Y. F., Gonzalez, C. G., & Harris, A. P. (Eds.). (2012). *Presumed innocent: The Intersections of race and class for women in academia*. University Press of Colorado.
Hull, A. (G. T.), Bell-Scott, P., & Smith, B. (Eds.). (1982/1993) *All the women are white, the Blacks are men, but some of us are brave*. The Feminist Press.
Kanter, R. M. (1977/1993). *Men and women of the corporation*. Basic.
Kellerman, B., & Rhode, D. (2014). Women at the top: the pipeline reconsidered. In K. A, Longman & S. R. Madsen (Eds.), *Women & leadership in higher education* (pp.3–22). Information Age.
National Center for Educational Statistics (NCES). (2019). Doctor's degrees conferred by postsecondary institutions, by race/ethnicity and sex of student: Selected years, 1976–77 through 2016–17. *Digest of Educational Statistics*. https://nces.ed.gov/programs/digest/d18/tables/dt18_324.20.asp
National Center for Education Statistics (NCES). (2020a). *Digest of Education Statistics. Table 324.30*. https://nces.ed.gov/programs/digest/d20/tables/dt20_324.20.asp
National Center for Education Statistics (NCES). (2020b). *Characteristics of post-secondary faculty*. https://nces.ed.gov/programs/coe/indicator/csc
National Center for Education Statistics (NCES). (2021). *Digest of Education Statistics: Table 315.10*. https://nces.ed.gov/programs/digest/d22/tables/dt22_315.10.asp
Niemann, Y. F., Gutiérrez y Muhs, G., & Gonzalez, C. G. (Eds.). (2020). *Presumed innocent II: Race, class, power, and resistance of women in academia*. University of Colorado.
Padillo, A. M. (1994). Ethnic minority scholars, research, and mentoring: Current and future issues. *Educational Researcher*, *23*(4), 24–27. https://doi.org/10.2307/1176259
Pratt-Clarke, M., & Maes, J. B. (Eds.). (2017). *Journeys of social justice: Women of color presidents in the academy*. Peter Lang.
Pratt-Clarke, M. (2017). Reflections from below the plantation roof. In M. Pratt-Clarke & J. B. Maes (Eds.), *Journeys of social justice: Women of color presidents in the academy* (pp. 11–30). Peter Lang.
Pyke, K. (2015). Faculty gender inequity and the "just say no to service" fairy tale. In K. De Welde & A. Stepnick (Eds.), *Disrupting the culture of silence: Confronting gender inequality and making change in higher education* (pp. 83–95). Stylus.
Sen, S. (2020). Women faculty of color face systemic oppression in America. *Visible*. https://visiblemagazine.com/women-faculty-of-color-face-systemic-oppression-in-academia/
Whitaker, H. C., & Grollman, E. A. (Eds.). (2018). *Counternarratives from women of color academics: Bravery, vulnerability, and resistance*. Routledge, Kindle ed.
Williams, J. (2015). The invisible labor of minority professors. In M. Pratt-Clarke & J. B. Maes (Eds.), *Journeys of social justice: Women of color presidents in the academy* (p. 7). Peter Lang.

4 Women's Leadership Journeys Across Sectors

Different Perspectives but the View Is the Same

Gail Simpson Cahill and Amy Rutstein-Riley

Framing the Context

Leadership should be about the work, not the power or recognition.

As long-standing participants of the LEAD group, we have a strong understanding of our own colleagues' lived experiences of leadership. However, to understand more fully the topic of women's leadership development, we thought it important to survey a larger sample of women leaders to understand more deeply their lived experiences of their professional work. As two long-term professors in higher education, we have an insider view of the culture of higher education and the opportunities and challenges for women in our own professional setting. Our perspective is informed solely by the institutions where we work and have built communities. To better understand the broader issue of women's leadership, it was important to branch out and look beyond our own colleagues and our university walls and consider the perspectives of women within and beyond the university setting. In this chapter, we seek to explore and reflect on the leadership development pathways of women in varied professions. We chose some that share similar gender profiles to higher education, such as PreK-12 education, and consider others such as STEM and business that share similarities and significant differences.

The paucity of women leaders in higher education is globally recognized today (Berry & Franks, 2010; Kruse, 2022). A visible challenge to women's leadership development trajectories is the lack of the consistent presence of role models, mentors, and sponsors. A less visible challenge, perhaps more difficult to pinpoint, is documented in a 2020 Harvard Business School publication, which notes that too many solutions seem founded on the misconception that women need to emulate men to be successful leaders. The article further argues that the challenge to advancing women is not a matter of the lack of competent females, but rather that there are too few obstacles for incompetent males ("7 leadership lessons men can learn from women," 2020).

DOI: 10.4324/9781003057208-4

The social and cultural conditions of the workplace continue to contribute to gender disparities in leadership. While often considered to be a problem at the individual level, such as a lack of training in leadership skills or innate drive, we contend that the dearth of women leaders is driven by structural challenges and obstacles placed in the way of women's achievement and leadership success. In this chapter, we have chosen to highlight four different professional fields represented by the 140 women who completed our survey: PreK-12 education, higher education, business, and STEM. A snapshot of the research and the themes from our survey underscore the importance of ongoing leadership development opportunities for women, such as those offered and supported by the LEAD approach. These learnings will inform our ongoing refinement and innovation of the LEAD methodology.

Framing the Research

PreK-12 Education

> *Having powerful female mentors and leaders to model after has helped me envision myself as a leader.*

In general, the status of professions continues to be gender biased and correlated with the number of men in the profession (Wong, 2019). It is not surprising, then, that the status of teachers remains low because of the number of women it attracts, especially in elementary schools (Wong, 2019). Public school teaching in grades Pre-Kindergarten to Grade 12 (PreK-12) remains primarily a women-dominated profession (Feistritzer et al., 2011; Grissom et al., 2013) with approximately 76% of teachers nationwide identifying as women (Wong, 2019). Despite the high number of women teachers, leadership positions remain male dominated (Fuller et al., 2018; Wong, 2019). It appears that the "glass escalator," a term first used by Williams (1992) to describe the rapid advancement of men, particularly white men, in primarily female-dominated professions such as health care and teaching continues to be evident in schools across our country.

Leadership research in PreK-12 education primarily focuses on the principalship and the superintendency. Burton and Weiner (2016) reported that 52% of PreK-8 principals are women whereas 30% of high school principals are women; according to a recent report of the New York Council of School Superintendents (NYCOSS), 81% of new superintendents came from a district position or a middle/high school principalship (Maranto et al., 2019; Ramaswamy, 2020). Despite a teaching workforce consisting of approximately 80% women, the highest rank of superintendency still remains a male dominated role with approximately one-quarter of the positions held by women (Maranto et al., 2018; Nuraan, 2018; Ramaswamy, 2020; Wong, 2019), and women of color remain "grossly" underrepresented with estimates as low as 2.2% of the nation's superintendents (Alston, 2005 as cited in Robinson et al., 2017, p. 1). Alston (2005) emphasized, "[i]n these United States, persons of color represent 10.9% of the nation's teachers, 12.3% of the nation's principals, but only 2.2% of the nation's superintendents" (p. 675). In addition, women principals and superintendents often report that they have been hired as instructional leaders in contrast to men who were most often hired as managers (Hallinger et al., 2016; Maranto et al., 2019).

Women leaders in education have identified support systems such as coaching, mentoring, and personal and professional networks as critical for their success (Gill, 2019; Maranto et al., 2019). Some school districts are beginning to provide support to women principals (Gill, 2019) and some organizations, such as the American Association of School Administrators (AASA), have recently launched initiatives to help women become superintendents by linking prospective women leaders with mentors (Superville, 2017). But more role models are needed (Ramaswamy, 2020). In addition, school districts need to explicitly conduct leadership searches that prioritize diversity of applicants to include women who identify as BIPOC as well as women who identify with a range of social identities (Grogan, 2005; Superville, 2017; Wiley et al., 2017). PreK-12 educational leadership programs, too, need to include coursework and the examination of implicit biases, structural inequality, and commitment to the advancement of members from marginalized communities (Burton & Weiner, 2016).

Higher Education

I don't think that it is natural for me to think of myself as a leader.

Since the late 1960s, and as a direct result of the civil rights movements and the women's movement, more women have entered higher education as students and professionals. Today, female students outnumber their male peers in undergraduate institutions (Bracken et al., 2023; Pasque & Simpson, 2013; "What's behind the growing gap between men and women in college completion?," 2021).

Graduate programs reflect a similar trend with women exceeding their male counterparts in a wide range of academic disciplines. Focusing on the PhD, women tend to complete programs in the areas of the arts, social sciences, or the helping professions including teaching and social work, in greater numbers than their male peers. In fact, since 2008–2009, women have earned a majority of doctoral degrees in each academic year and in increasingly more academic areas (Gammel & Rutstein-Riley, 2016; "What's behind the growing gap between men and women in college completion?," 2021). The statistics become more complicated, however, when social identities of race, ethnicity, and social class intersect with gender (Fast facts: Degrees conferred by race/ethnicity and sex (72)," n.d.).

For women faculty, the leadership trajectory in the higher education workspace is fraught with organizational and structural barriers as examined in Chapter 3. For example, pathways toward promotion and tenure and women's progression into senior leadership positions can be challenging. Women can languish at the Associate Professor rank because of work life balance while negotiating the *second shift* (Hochschild & Machung, 2012). Since March 2020, the COVID pandemic has made visible the tremendous multifaceted burdens women faculty negotiate on a daily basis. Securing grant funding, supervising labs and graduate students, and teaching and service requirements, when balanced against personal demands in the private domain such as childcare, parental care, and the responsibilities of "the sandwich generation" more often fall on the shoulders of women as compared to men, often resulting in a slowed progression toward the rank of Professor, a status typically required for crossing into the senior leadership lane. This reality is further complicated when we look at this issue through the lens of race, ethnicity, and social class. It is well known that faculty who identify as BIPOC often receive more negative course evaluations relative to their white peers reflecting implicit bias on the part of students completing evaluations, while white male faculty often receive the highest ratings ("Just a moment.," n.d.). Furthermore, marital status similarly complicates the leadership trajectory for women faculty amplifying the tension between family responsibilities and demands of the academy.

The pandemic has highlighted the ongoing stressors and need for support and leadership development for women faculty, department chairs, deans and other senior leaders. The demands placed upon women faculty and leaders during the pandemic resulted in many women teaching their university classes while also homeschooling their children and caring for family members. The pandemic also resulted in the slowing of scholarly productivity and service contributions required for advancement in rank. These unexpected simultaneous pressures to flip to virtual instruction and work from home while supporting family members resulted in many women foregoing their professional development in a variety of areas including the area of leadership. This reality disproportionately negatively impacted women's advancement in the higher education context (Lafkas et al., 2023). In addition, recent simultaneous pressures in the higher education space – enrollment and fiscal challenges, college and university reorganization efforts, shifting student demographics, the return to in person learning post COVID 19, and an increasingly contentious learning environment where civil discourse and DEI initiatives are fracturing, has resulted in even greater pressures on university faculty and leadership leading to burnout (Pope-Ruark, 2022), dissatisfaction, and a shift in the perception of the value of the work of teaching and learning in the academy. All of these very real shifting factors combined with an increasingly negative public perception of the value of higher education. All of these variables contribute to women's decisions to consider to enter into and/or depart from the leadership space in the academy.

Today, there is a considerable push to advance women into the Cabinet level (C-suite) of colleges and universities. For example, the American Council of Education (ACE) has a national program devoted to "moving the needle: advancing women in higher education leadership" that was established in 2014 to advance women into presidential positions with, "the vision is to achieve gender parity in the percentage of higher education chief executives by 2030" ("Moving the needle: Advancing women in higher education leadership," n.d.). In response to a real need to advance women in higher education, organizations have responded both internally and externally to the demands of quality leadership professional development. Many universities, for example, have internal programs established through the Provost's office as well Human Resources to support the advancement of women in their institutions. In addition, there are several long-standing, externally well-known leadership development programs for women in higher education including The HERS Institute, the Yale School of Management (SOM) Executive Education Women's Leadership Program, and Women in Education Leadership Program (Harvard Graduate School of Education), to name a few programs. While these programs are popular and effective, they can be cost prohibitive for many who may wish to participate. As colleges and universities tighten their purse strings, it becomes challenging to find financial support necessary to participate in such offerings. This was part of the challenge at Lesley University, which became the backdrop of the impetus to form the LEADership group.

Business

Women are expected to deliver despite the lack of resources.

The absence of women in the Boardroom and at the helm of companies, commonly known as the C-suite (e.g., CEO, CFO), continues to highlight the limited progress women have carved into positions of power and influence in the business sector (Berry & Franks, 2010). Global research reports that women make up only 3% of positions at the executive level, despite the many studies that have shown their performance to be the same, if not better, than their male counterparts (Kooskora & Piigli, 2015). A comparison of 100 Fortune 500 companies between 2001 and 2011, for example, found that women executives were promoted faster than men, but this advantage disappeared once companies secured one high ranking woman executive (Bonet et al., 2020) despite the fact that companies who promote women tend to outpace their competition on every profitability measure researched (Coates, 2016; Johns, 2013).

There is a deluge of research literature devoted to the importance of mentorship and sponsorship, albeit the latter research is more sparse, to advance women into positions of power and influence proffered by other women. The demand for women-to-women mentorship programs abounds in all business sectors – entrepreneurship, finance, and manufacturing to name only a few (Bullough et al., 2015; Fry, 2014; Segarra, 2011; Sharafizad, 2018). The supply, however, falls short with over half of the companies surveyed not offering any programs for mentoring only women (Castellano, 2015; Ward, 2016). In general, mentorship programs are touted to foster the development of all women, whereas sponsorship appears to be most effective for promoting women into specific employment or high-visibility work (Segarra, 2011). It is anticipated that e-mentoring platforms will tackle the barrier of too few women to mentor or sponsor other women by reducing some of the challenges associated with male mentorships when few women mentors are available in an organization (Rockwell et al., 2013).

Successful women mentorship programs in business such as NetSuite and PayPal highlight several considerations for the future development of similar programs (Ward, 2016). For example, Recruiterbox Inc., a company devoted to hiring personnel, suggests first forming a leadership group to facilitate the group's unfolding and continuation. Then, all women in the organization should be invited to participate as a mentor or a mentee. Finally, goals should be established to judge the effectiveness of the program over time such as the increase of women's representation in management and the tracking of mentee promotions (Recruiterbox Inc., n.d.). Size of the group is important as well, too large and mentorship efforts often fail (Ward, 2016). Many businesses are also working directly with companies such as Catalyst, a global nonprofit company that aims to build workplaces that support women (*About Us,* 2023*). Technology has also integrated itself into mentorship. Amazon, for example, recently teamed with the cloud-based mentoring platform Chronous to match mentors with mentees in their organization in the hopes of building a more inclusive workplace (Schomer, 2022).*

Ultimately, the overarching goal for companies is to build a culture of mentorship that shapes an organization's capacity, competency, and capability (Johnson, 2014). And, for women of color, access to assignments that are highly visible and critical should be a strategic priority (Pace, 2018).

STEM

Too many men making the decisions . . . structural sexism.

The future job growth areas in the United States are currently projected to be in the STEM fields (Nilanjana & Stout, 2014; Piazza and Harvey Mudd College, 2012). A robust job market for graduates is predicted, yet the number of women entering these fields continues to lag behind their male counterparts (Piazza and Harvey Mudd College, 2012), in part due to gender stereotyping that men are better prepared to succeed in STEM related disciplines thus handicapping the number of girls who were encouraged to pursue these fields (Allison & Cossette, 2007).

Today there is purposeful activity to attract young girls and women (Palid et al., 2023). The question, then, is how best to attract and retain women in the STEM fields?

The research literature documents that barriers exist to the development of interest in STEM fields at every life stage of a woman's development (Milgram, 2011; Nilanjana & Stout, 2014). Multiple interventions at all stages of development are, therefore, recommended (Milgram, 2011; Nilanjana & Stout, 2014). One suggestion is to augment the collaborations between PreK-12 schools and youth serving organizations and women role models to include women of color in STEM departments in colleges and universities as well as in the workplace (Ilumoka et al., 2017; Milgram, 2011; Nilanjana & Stout, 2014). Another suggestion is to initiate a robust national outreach campaign, which has been shown to be effective in the past, as with the Rosie the Riveter campaign of World War II (Milgram, 2011). The goal is to increase interest and women need to feel confident in their abilities before their interest can be boosted (Allison & Cossette, 2007).

Same-gender mentoring is the most often cited strategy to recruit and support women in the STEM fields. Counselors in PreK-12 schools and colleges can support women with information about careers, training, and the implementation of various mentoring supports from cross-generational to 1:1 peer mentoring (Allison & Cossette, 2007; Brookover et al., 2021). Higher education is encouraged to promote a more inclusive culture to recruit, retain, and promote women (Fridkis-Hareli, 2011), as well as to remove any organizational constraints that lead to gender bias in the hiring and promotion of women STEM faculty (Laursen et al., 2015; Nilanjana & Stout, 2014). One successful national mentoring program is the Association for Women in Science (AWIS), an organization that provides a supportive environment for women to gain leadership experience and discuss workplace issues (Fridkis-Hareli, 2011). Local programs are also gaining momentum throughout the country. Two programs at the university where we work are the *STEM Learning* labs, which support local educators and students, and the *WonderLab*, a 21st century model for university lab schools. One caution in the STEM literature, because it is still highly male dominant, is the potential for women's mentoring programs to fall short because they may unwittingly reinforce gender inequality and male dominance by appearing that women need support to advance and males do not need added support (Williams et al., 2014). We postulate that until parity for women in STEM fields is achieved, mentoring and sponsoring women in science are essential.

A Survey of Leaders: What Did We Learn?

We developed and administered a survey to women leaders to enhance our understanding of the current literature on gender parity and equity in higher education, PreK-12 public education, business, and STEM fields, with an emphasis on higher education. The survey can be found at the end of this chapter. It consisted of 36 questions including Likert-scaled items, closed questions, and open-ended questions. Participants were recruited through professional organizations and personal affiliations and were encouraged to share the survey with colleagues, which produced a snowball sampling effect.

The survey yielded 140 respondents, 80% of whom work in higher education; the remaining 20% were scattered among PreK-12 schools, business, and STEM careers. The average age fell within the 50- to 59 year category. Most respondents self-identified as white (88%) and the other 12% identified as Black or African American (6%), Latinx (3%), or Asian (3%). All respondents reported that they accepted their first formal leadership role before the age of 50.

Powerful female mentors and leaders to model after has helped me envision myself as a leader.

A *mentor*, for purposes of this survey, was defined as *a person who gives you help and advice over a period of time related to your job and career*. An overwhelming majority (85%) of respondents reported that most of their support was found outside of work; only 15% of the study's participants had support groups at their place of employment. Approximately 80% of respondents stated they had an unofficial mentor albeit only 5% had a mentor at their current workplace. Some respondents had a *sponsor*, defined as *a person who helps you position yourself to get promoted in your organization and/or advance in your career,* but in far fewer numbers; roughly 40% of respondents identified a sponsor from either inside or outside their organization. Both mentorship and sponsorship are important to the professional leadership development trajectories of the women surveyed, with most important mentoring and sponsoring relationships occurring beyond the physical workplace in informal spaces. Thus, it is particularly important to make visible networks of opportunities for women outside the workspace, so that women may develop mentoring and sponsoring relationships. If these relationships are not organically developed at work, the places where they can be found, facilitated, and fostered need to be transparent and accessible for women.

My largest barrier is me. I often doubt if I can 'go that far'.

The majority of respondents (92%) recognized barriers or obstacles that limited their advancement to leadership roles. Some barriers were structural such as finite leadership development opportunities or political, "politics within the organization." Other barriers were personal or internal, "fear of success"; "lack of confidence"; and "aversion to conflict." In contrast, the primary factor cited by a majority of respondents to support leadership advancement was the presence of mentors, "Amazing mentors that have believed in me, guided me and told me difficult truths," and "Having powerful female mentors and leaders to model." In addition to mentors, other strategies to overcome advancement obstacles were meditation, self-reflection, prayer, sense of humor, professional development, joining committees, reading, attending leadership conferences, and obtaining advanced degrees such as a "doctorate" or an "MBA."

The respondents were asked about further development to advance, change, or augment their current professional roles. Some respondents desired more technical skills in project management, finance, fundraising, and leadership training. Others requested training on the "soft skills": "I feel that we always need training on the soft skills – how to manage, how to have a difficult conversation." Several respondents mentioned a personal coach or mentor to help them better manage a work-life balance. A continued struggle for many respondents centered on the development of their voice: "I am interested in learning how administrators can value female qualities of leadership"; and "not having to fight for my value at the senior level of administration." As one respondent stated, "I feel that women are always asked to be assistant/associate and are not acknowledged at the workplace. Junior male colleagues are disrespectful and not supportive. They have stereotypes about minority women."

She saw something in me I didn't see in myself.

Many sources of influence on respondents' pursuit of leadership positions were noted. Many cited a boss or a mentor, "My previous boss, the first boss to promote me to a leadership/management role. She saw something in me I didn't see in myself." Others spoke in general terms, "Seeing women like myself stepping up to positions and blossoming themselves and their organizations thriving." Family members were also credited in responses: "My spouse who has always encouraged me . . ."; "My family – I want to be a good model for my children and grandchildren"; and "My grandmother was a mother of seven who worked in the mills to support her family. She demonstrated resilience, leadership, and drive. She passed that along to my mother, who was also driven, compassionate and successful. The legacy of these strong role models has pushed me to achieve and grow."

One respondent, however, could not identify an influence on her success, "Sad to say, I really do not have one. I feel like this has been an uphill battle on my own and it is frustrating."

People around me recognized leadership qualities that I didn't see in myself.

The respondents were asked to share a brief story of a time or event when they recognized themselves as a leader; most, however, shared stories of recognition from others because for most of the participants the outer voice held more power than the inner self knowledge: "I don't think that it is natural for me to think of myself as a leader. Rather, it is when other people use that term for me that I can see myself through their eyes." Others shared similar thoughts, "My boss recognized my leadership skills."; "Being asked to serve."; "When I was nominated."; and "I was appointed."

Confidence, connections, perseverance.

Respondents were asked to give a piece of advice to another woman wanting to advance into a leadership position. Most responses focused on self-belief: "Believe in yourself"; "Give it a try – take the leap"; "Share the fact that you want to advance in your career. Don't wait for others to notice." Respondents also encouraged other women to connect with others and ask for help, "My advice would be to understand that you do not operate in a vacuum and to take advantage of relationships with colleagues and friends in the industry." Several respondents advised women to "support other women"; "Lift other women up," and, "don't go for leadership roles just for the sake of rising in the ranks." Finally, the theme of perseverance came through in many responses, as one respondent summarized, "Do not give up, persevere, AND never let them see you cry – both men and women see that as weakness. Until there are enough female leaders, we have to prove that we are as strong or stronger than our male contemporaries."

Relatedly, when asked to share actions that they found to be most beneficial to their pursuit of leadership, many argued that it was important to sometimes apply for and/or take positions that were, "slightly beyond my wheelhouse of comfort" or "out of my league" in order to grow in experience. Others suggested that women not wait for the "perfect" position or the "right" age, but rather learn to take risks. Several respondents stated that a "willingness to move" was helpful to ascend into leadership positions. Personal relationships were also noted as being supportive or impeding leadership ascent, "I chose a leadership position over a relationship with my partners (twice)."

I began to lead/direct my own life, rather than be led.

The final question asked respondents to reflect on an event or turning point in their development as a leader. Responses ranged from "SO many" to "I can't think of one in particular." Some events or experiences that respondents believed helped their development included: "stepping down from a job when I lost the support of my constituents"; "getting let go of a job or not getting a job for reasons that had nothing to do with my performance"; "left a job because I worked for unethical leaders and decided I needed to be true to my convictions"; or "made the decision to get a divorce. It was when I finally decided that my feelings, my needs were more important than anyone else's . . . I began to lead/direct my own life, rather than be led."

For most respondents, it appeared that their leadership development was just that, a process of starts and stops, hurts and laughter, and wins and losses,

> It was a gradual development. Collaboration and cooperation are key. You can't stand alone. Learn to cultivate relationships, every person at every level of the organization plays an important role. Never shut off someone because you don't think they have enough clout. You are only a leader if others think you are a leader.

We were overwhelmed by the sheer number of women who opted to respond to this fairly lengthy survey (n = 140 respondents). Perhaps our response rate reflects a desire to share one's story, or perhaps little opportunity to reflect upon one's own leadership development journey. Our participants reflected a range of professional roles and backgrounds, and the themes from the responses presented highlight a complex and complicated road for women leaders. Offering women opportunities for strong mentorship, sponsorship, and professional development is both necessary and the right thing to do to empower women in the workplace and in the culture of leadership. It is interesting to note that many of our survey respondents spoke about personal motivations, opportunities, and challenges to their leadership journeys and did not particularly highlight the structural inequalities inherent in the professions to which they belong. This may be a flaw in the survey design or perhaps a function of age, life stage, gender socialization, as well as the reflective process. In future research on this issue, it would be important to explore the explicit beliefs of women leaders on structural inequities built into the professions and how the design of organizational cultures impacts the lived experiences and perceptions of leadership among women leaders.

Lessons Learned: What Can a LEAD Approach Do?

> *"Lift other women up."*

The intentional design of LEAD reflects the research on women's leadership development, as reported earlier in the chapter and in Chapter 1, and we see strong connection between the themes identified in the data presented in this chapter and the LEAD method and group process. The LEAD group provided support to women in the form of mentorship, connectivity, and relational problem-solving, and did so through self-exploration and examination of deeply embedded structural inequities based on gender and other social identities we hold; we actively focused on the individual, the sociopolitical, and the intersections among the two. A group with longevity and consistency of membership, such as LEAD, also provided an ongoing space for group members to grow in relationship with each other, to believe in each other, and to be the givers and receivers of support for the LEAD members over the course of their leadership journeys. Over time, we supported the growth of individual members as they moved into specific institutional leadership roles, such as Chair, Dean, and Vice Provost. Collectively we sought to develop needed leadership expertise through participation in LEAD and together we co-constructed new leadership knowledge, competence, confidence, and voice. We supported each other in words and actions both within the LEAD group space and in meetings and committees we inhabited, each strengthened by the collaborative strategic leadership moves cultivated within our group. The themes highlighted from the survey data align with the design of LEAD, most notably an intentional focus on self and peer and mentorship, self and group exploration, relational leadership strategies, and development of leader identity among our group members. For LEAD participants, the role of peer support and mentorship in the context of a relational space where leadership as a concept and practice was explored facilitated the internal development of confidence, a sense of competence, and voice, resulting in a vision of self-as-leader.

Survey

Demographics

1. What field best describes your leadership work?
   a. Higher education
   b. PreK-12 education
   c. Business
   d. Medicine
   e. STEM
   f. Other: please explain
2. What is your current age grouping?
   a. Under 30
   b. 31–40
   c. 41–50
   d. 51–60
   e. 61–70
   f. 70+
3. Do you identify as . . .? (Please check all that apply)
   a. Latina/Latinx
   b. American Indian or Alaska Native
   c. Asian
   d. Black or African American
   e. Native Hawaiian or Other Pacific Islander
   f. White
   g. Mixed race/ethnicity
   h. I do not choose to answer

4. At what age did you first consider yourself a leader?*

    a. Under 18
    b. 18–24
    c. 25–30
    d. 31–40
    e. 41–50
    f. 51–60
    g. 61–70
    h. 70+

5. What age did you first accept a formal leadership role in your professional work?

    a. Under 30
    b. 31–40
    c. 41–50
    d. 51–60
    e. 61–70
    f. 70+

6. How many leadership positions have you held?

    a. 1
    b. 2–3
    c. 4–6
    d. 7–9
    e. 10 or more

7. How long have you been in your current position?

    a. Less than 1 year
    b. 1–3 years
    c. 4–6 years
    d. 7–9 years
    e. Over ten years, please specify the number of years

8. Do you hold a degree or certificate in administration/leadership/management?

    a. Yes*
    b. No

    *If yes, please list your credential(s):

9. How large is your entire organization?

    a. Less than 50 employees
    b. 51–249
    c. 250–499
    d. 500–999

  e. 1000–4,999
  f. Over 5000

10. Do you belong to any current women leadership support groups? (Please check all that apply)

  a. Yes at the workplace*
  b. No at the workplace
  c. Yes outside of the workplace*
  d. None
  e. *If yes, please identify the group(s):

11. Have you switched industries throughout your leadership development? If so, please explain.

The next few questions ask about a mentor, which we define as a person who gives you help and advice over a period of time related to your job and career.

12. Do you identify anyone as a mentor?

  a. Yes
  b. No

13. Do you have an official mentor in your organization?

  a. Yes

     What is the role of the person?

  b. No

14. Do you have an unofficial mentor in your organization?

  a. Yes

     What is the role of the person?

  b. No

The next few questions ask about a **sponsor**, which we define as a person who helps you position yourself to get promoted in your organization and/or to advance in your career.

15. Do you identify anyone as a sponsor in your organization?

  a. Yes*
  b. No

     If yes, please provide an example of their sponsorship.

16. Do you identify anyone outside your organization as a sponsor?

    a. Yes*
    b. No

    If yes, please provide an example of their sponsorship.

Leadership Development

A. **(Likert Scale)**

Please rate your responses:
(Likert scale: 1–4–1: strongly disagree; 2: disagree; 3: agree; 4: strongly agree)

1. There are opportunities to develop women for leadership roles at my place of work.
2. I would be interested in receiving more leadership development at my place of work.
3. I believe having a mentor helps me/would help me pursue my leadership aspirations.
4. I think strategically about my own leadership development.
5. I have a written or informal professional development plan that supports my growth as a leader.
6. I am aware of the barriers or obstacles that could stand in the way of advancing in my career in my organization.
7. Vendors, or outside consultants, are used to develop all or parts of development programs for women leaders at my employment.
8. My workplace uses strategies to create a recruiting process that is inclusive of gender and diversity.
9. My workplace has a budget for leadership development and inclusion programs dedicated to women in leadership and gender equity efforts.
10. I have pursued other opportunities or places for leadership development.
11. I maintain a balance between my personal and professional life.

B. Open-Ended questions

1. Can you share a brief story of a time or event when you first recognized yourself as a leader?
2. What are the 2–3 most important factors that have helped you develop as a leader?
3. What do you consider to be barriers to your own leadership development or opportunities for achievement?
4. Please list 1–2 things you have done to overcome obstacles to your leadership practice.

5. In what areas would you like more development to advance, change, or augment your current professional role?
6. What or whom do you consider the greatest influence on your pursuit of a leadership position and why?
7. If you could give one piece of advice to another woman wanting to advance into a leadership position, what would it be?
8. Throughout your life and career, what 2–3 actions that you chose to take have been the most significant in your pursuit of leadership?
9. Has there been an event or turning point in your development as a leader that you can identify as critical to your view of self as a leader? If so, please explain.

References

7 leadership lessons men can learn from women. (2020, April 1). *Harvard business review*. https://hbr.org/2020/04/7-leadership-lessons-men-can-learn-from-women?utm_source=twitter&utm_medium=social&utm_campaign=hbr

About Us: Catalyst. (2023, April 11). Retrieved May 7, 2023, from https://www.catalyst.org/mission/

Allison, C., & Cossette, I. (2007). Theory and practice in recruiting women for STEM careers. *Proceedings of the 2007 WEPAN National Conference, 21*. https://www.semanticscholar.org/paper/Theory-and-Practice-in-Recruiting-Women-for-STEM-Allison-Cossette/898ea729a333e27f512a34e0f6e5af9ad61b7b61

Alston, J. A. (2005). Tempered radicals and servant leaders: Black females persevering in the superintendency. *Educational Administration Quarterly, 41*(5), 675–688. https://doi.org/10.1177/0013161X04274275

Berry, P., & Franks, T. J. (2010). Women in the world of corporate business: Looking at the glass ceiling. *Contemporary Issues in Education Research (CIER), 3*(2), 1–10. https://doi.org/10.19030/cier.v3i2.171

Bonet, R., Cappelli, P., & Hamori, M. (2020). Gender differences in speed of advancement: An empirical examination of top executives in the Fortune 100 firms. *Strategic Management Journal* (John Wiley & Sons, Inc.), *41*(4), 708–737. https://doi-org.ezproxyles.flo.org/10.1002/smj.3125

Bracken, S. J., Allen, J. K., Sadker, D., & Dean, D. R. (2023). *Most college students are women: Implications for teaching learning and policy*. https://doi.org/10.4324/9781003446064

Brookover, D., Livingston, A., & Cartwright, I. (2021). "It's never too late": High school counselors' support of underrepresented students' interest in STEM. *The Professional Counselor, 11*(2), 143. https://doi-org.ezproxyles.flo.org/10.15241/alc.11.2.143

Bullough, A., De Luque, M. S., Abdelzaher, D., & Heim, W. (2015). Developing women leaders through entrepreneurship education and training. *Academy of Management Perspectives, 29*(2), 250–270. https://doi.org/10.5465/amp.2012.0169

Burton, L. J., & Weiner, J. M. (2016). "They were really looking for a male leader for the building": Gender, identity and leadership development in a principal preparation program. *Frontiers in Psychology, 7*. https://doi.org/10.3389/fpsyg.2016.00141

Castellano, S. (2015). Girl talk. *TD: Talent Development, 69*(6), 10.

Coates, M. (2016). Women's programs are far from being a favor. *PRWeek (U.S. Edition), 19*(4), 39.

Fast facts: Degrees conferred by race/ethnicity and sex (72). (n.d.). *National Center for Education Statistics (NCES), a part of the U.S. department of education.* https://nces.ed.gov/fastfacts/display.asp?id=72

Feistritzer, C. E., Griffin, S., & Linnajarvi, A. (2011). *Profile of teachers in the US*. National Center for Education Information.

Fridkis-Hareli, M. (2011). A mentoring program for women scientists meets a pressing need. *Nature Biotechnology, 29*(3), 287–288. https://doi.org/10.1038/nbt.1799

Fry, M. (2014). Gender still a factor in the manufacturing world. *Njbiz, 27*(25), 14.

Fuller, E. J., Pendola, A., & LeMay, M. (2018). Who should be our leader? Examining female representation in the principalship across geographic locales in Texas public schools. *Journal of Research in Rural Education, 34*(4). Rhttps://search.ebscohost.com/login.aspx?direct=true&db=eric&AN=EJ1172797&site=eds-live&scope=site

Gammel, J., & Rutstein-Riley, A. (2016). A relational approach to mentoring doctoral students. *New Directions for Teaching and Learning, 147*, 27–35. https://doi.org/10.1002AL20196

Gill, J. (2019). Lean on me: To help principals become better instructional leaders, districts are boosting on-the-job supports such as mentoring and coaching. *Educational Leadership, 76*(6), 43.

Grissom, J. A., Loeb, S., & Master, B. (2013). Effective instructional time use for school leaders: Longitudinal evidence from observations of principals. *Educ. Res., 42*, 433–444. https://doi.org/10.3102/0013189X13510020

Grogan, M. (2005). Echoing their ancestors, women lead school districts in the United States. *International Studies in Educational Administration, 33*(2), 21–30. https://search.ebscohost.com/login.aspx?direct=true&db=aph&AN=19363500&site=eds-live&scope=site

Hallinger, P., Dongyu, L., & Wang, W-C. (2016) Gender differences in instructional leadership: A meta-analytic review of studies using the principal instructional management rating scale. *Educational Administration Quarterly, 52*(4), 567–601. https://doi.org/10.1177/0013161X16638430

Hochschild, A., & Machung, A. (2012). *The second shift: Working families and the revolution at home*. Penguin.

Ilumoka, A., Milanovic, I., & Grant, N. (2017). An effective industry-based mentoring approach for the recruitment of women and minorities in engineering. *Journal of STEM Education: Innovations and Research, 18*(3), 13–19.

Johns, M. L. (2013). Breaking the glass ceiling: Structural, cultural, and organizational barriers preventing women from achieving senior and executive positions. *Perspectives in Health Information Management, 10*(Winter), 1e.

Johnson, B. O. (2014). Business mentoring. *Business People*, 62. https://www.chronicle.com/article/teaching-evaluations-are-broken-can-they-be-fixed

Kooskora, M., & Piigli, M. (2015). Discussion of the leadership profile of female top executives. *Journal of Management & Change, 34/35*(1/2), 107–122.

Kruse, S. (2022). "I am the chair": Women and department leadership in the academy. *Frontiers in Education, 7*. https://doi-org.ezproxyles.flo.org/10.3389/feduc.2022.814581

Lafkas, S. M., Christensen, M., & Madsen, S. R. (2023). The impact of COVID-19 on women and work: Career advancement challenges. *Merits, 3(*1), 167–185. https://doi.org/10.3390/merits3010011

Laursen, S. L., Austin, A. E., Soto, M., & Martinez, D. (2015). ADVANCing the agenda for gender equity. *Change: The Magazine of Higher Learning, 47*(4), 16–23.

Maranto, R., Carroll, K., Cheng, A., & Teodoro, M. P. (2018). Boys will be superintendents: School leadership as a gendered profession: Why do men still fill most district leadership positions, and what can be done about it? *Phi Delta Kappan*, (2). https://search.ebscohost.com/login.aspx?direct=true&db=edsgbc&AN=edsgcl.562866802&site=e ds-live&scope=site

Maranto, R., Teodoro, M. P., Carroll, K., & Cheng, A. (2019). Gendered ambition: Men's and women's career advancement in public administration. *American Review of Public Administration*, *49*(4), 469.

Milgram, D. (2011). How to recruit women and girls to the Science, Technology, Engineering, and Math (STEM) classroom. *Technology and Engineering Teacher*, *71*(3), 4–11.

Moving the needle: Advancing women in higher education leadership. (n.d.). *American council on education*. https://www.acenet.edu/Programs-Services/Pages/Communities/Moving-the-Needle.aspx

Nilanjana D., & Stout, J. (2014). Girls and women in science, technology, engineering, and mathematics: STEMing the tide and broadening participation in STEM careers. *Policy Insights from the Behavioral and Brain Sciences*, *1*(1), 21–29. https://doi.org/10.1177/2372732214549471

Nuraan, D. (2018). *The mercury (South Africa)*. https://search.ebscohost.com/login.aspx?direct=true&db=edsgwh&AN=edsgcl.548744757&site=eds-live&scope=site

Pace, C. (2018). How women of color get to senior management. In *Harvard business review*. Harvard Business School Publishing Corporation.

Palid, O., Cashdollar, S., Deangelo, S., Chu, C., & Bates, M. (2023). Inclusion in practice: A systematic review of diversity-focused STEM programming in the United States. *International Journal of STEM Education*, *10*(1), 1–16. https://doi-org.ezproxyles.flo.org/10.1186/s40594-022-00387-3

Pasque, P., & Simpson, E. (2013). Women's status in higher education: Equity matters by Elizabeth J. Allan (review). *The Review of Higher Education*, *36*(3), 426–427. https://doi.org/10.1353/rhe.2013.0032

Piazza and Harvey Mudd College Launch First Online Community Mentorship Program to Support STEM Women. (2012, September 17). *Internet wire*. https://www.hmc.edu/about-hmc/category/harvey-mudd-in-the-news/

Pope-Ruark. (2022). *Unraveling faculty burnout: Pathways to reckoning and renewal*. John Hopkins University Press.

Ramaswamy, S. (2020, August 3). School superintendents are overwhelmingly male: What's holding women back from the top job? *The Journal News*. https://https://www.usatoday.com/story/news/education/2020/02/20/female-school-district-superintendents-westchester-rockland/4798754002/

Recruiterbox, Inc. (n.d.). *How to create a women's mentorship program in your company*. https://hire.trakstar.com/business-guides/women-in-business/create-womens-mentorship-program-in-your-company

Robinson, K., Shakeshaft, C., Grogen, M., & Sherman Newcomb, W. (2017). Necessary but not sufficient: The continuing inequality between men and women in educational leadership, findings from the American association of School administrators mid-decade study. *Frontiers in Education*, *2*(12). https://doi.org/10,3389/feduc.2017.00012

Rockwell, B. V., Leck, J. D., & Elliott, C. J. (2013). Can e-mentoring take the "gender" out of mentoring? *Cyberpsychology*, *7*(2), 1–11. https://doi.org/10.5817/CP2013-2-5

Schomer, S. (2022, October 12). Amazon is upskilling its workers via mentoring. *PlatforChronus*. Employee Benefit News. Retrieved May 7, 2023, from https://www.benefitnews.com/news/amazon-is-upskilling-workers-via-mentoring-platform-chronus

Segarra, M. (2011). Talking the next step. *CFO*, *27*(6), 60–66.

Sharafizad, J. (2018). Informal learning of women small business owners. *Education & Training*, *60*(1), 82–103.

Superville, D. (2017). Few women run the nation's school districts: Why? Stubborn gender gap in the top job. *Education Week, 36*(13), 10–13.

Ward, K. (2016, October 10). These companies run mentorship programs that actually work. *Fast Company*. https://www.fastcompany.com/3064292/these-companies-run-mentorship-Programs-that-actually-work

What's behind the growing gap between men and women in college completion? (2021, November 8). *Pew research center*. https://www.pewresearch.org/short-reads/2021/11/08/whats-behind-the-growing-gap-between-men-and-women-in-college-completion/

Wiley, K., Bustamante, R., Ballenger, J., & Polnick, B. (2017). African American women superintendents in Texas: an exploration of challenges and supports. *Journal of School Administration Research and Development, 2*(1), 18–24.

Williams, C. L. (1992). The glass escalator: Hidden advantages for men in the "female" professions. *Social Problems, 39*(3), 253–267. https://doi.org/10.1525/sp.1992.39.3.03x0034h

Williams, C. L., Kilanski, K., & Muller, C. (2014). Corporate diversity programs and gender inequality in the oil and gas industry. *Work & Occupations, 41*(4), 440–476. https://doi.org/10.1177/0730888414539172

Wong, A. (2019, February 20). The U.S. teaching population is getting bigger, and more female. *The Atlantic*. https://www.theatlantic.com/education/archive/2019/02/the explosion-of-women-teachers/582622/

5 Mentoring as an Act of Leadership

Barbara Govendo

Introduction

Mentoring is an age-old approach to learning. Blacksmiths, potters, bootmakers, and weavers learned their crafts through mentoring apprenticeships. Medical, financial, and educational fields presently have an extended approach to learning, both in the classroom and in a practical setting through internships and residencies. In higher education, mentoring is seen as an important facet of becoming a successful faculty member and leader (De Welde & Stepnick, 2015; Seltzer, 2015).

Trends of the past several decades demonstrate the notable increases in degree attainment for women of all racial/ethnic groups in the United States. Women now earn more degrees than men in all levels of post-secondary education, including even in some fields at the doctoral level (Bierema, 2017). Public policy since the 1970s would seem to have mitigated some of the discrimination in hiring and promotion that women have historically faced in the United States. Women have increased their presence in faculty positions across the United States to today comprising almost 43% of all tenured or tenure-track faculty positions (AAUP Update, 2020). All these factors, however, have not led to a significant movement of women into senior positions of leadership in higher education.

The question of why women have not moved more steadily into senior leadership in higher education is puzzling. Women's experience of opportunities for leadership in higher education, their lived experience as faculty, and their opportunities for advancement in leadership must all be understood as shaped by powerful and complex organizational, social, and cultural factors, including complex and interrelated barriers. While my research and writing in this project touches on these barriers to women's successful movement into senior positions of higher education leadership in the United States today, the focus of this chapter is the mentoring experiences of women in higher education faculty or leadership positions in order to illuminate the effects of mentoring on their careers. Implications for successful mentoring activities or leadership development programs will be suggested.

DOI: 10.4324/9781003057208-5

Barriers to Women in Senior Leadership

Men have historically been mentored with an eye towards "moving up the ladder." Women do not always have that type of mentoring. Many women who have succeeded in making their way to the top have done so because men in leadership positions have seen their promise and have supported them in their rise. More often, women are not encouraged to apply for higher positions or are actively discouraged from moving upward or passed over despite their skills or readiness. Gender stereotypes may interfere with acknowledgement of a woman's skills and abilities (Keohane, 2014).

There are often differences between the way male faculty members are mentored and female faculty members are mentored. Seltzer (2015) describes the difference between a sponsor relationship versus a mentor relationship as having better results for men who are sponsored leading to promotion versus women who are mentored and supported by those who may not be as powerful in the organization. Mentor relationships help the mentees learn their way around, gain practical skills, and feel comfortable in their positions within the organization. Sponsor relationships support the development of skills and personnel but also actively promote the individuals to others in positions of authority or higher decision-making.

White (2014) cites the reluctance of women to take positions of leadership – even when offered – due to workplace realities unique to women, for example, demands of position made harder by expectations of women leaders, lack of support by institutions of higher learning for their women's family commitments, lack of opportunity for women of color to be chosen for presidencies.

Types of Mentor Relationships

Despite the difficulties women face in rising to leadership positions and their reluctance to accept positions when offered, mentoring is still seen as a productive and effective approach for supporting faculty success as well as career and leadership development.

Murphy et al. (2017) suggest that there are five types of developmental relationships for women as they move into higher leadership positions: mentors, sponsors, peers, executive coaches, and learning partners. These types of relationships, along with relational mentoring, will be further discussed and illustrated later.

Mentors

Mentoring relationships enable the mentee to navigate the educational institution. Mentoring, as defined by Meschitti and Smith (2017), "implies an exclusive relationship in which a more experienced person provides strategic advice to facilitate the professional and personal development of another, less experienced one" (p. 167).

Bland et al. (2009) suggest methods of supporting women who are interested in pursuing leadership positions in academia, for example, clarifying skills needed for chosen positions, developing strategies to strengthen those particular skills, sharing examples of responsibilities, schedules and routines of those in leadership positions.]

As will be illustrated below in my interviews with executive and faculty leaders at Lesley University, informal mentoring relationships can be as important or more important in a mentee's development as more formal ones, as noted by Murphy et al. (2017). Often, informal mentors who are chosen for particular knowledge, skills, or attributes are more significant than the more formal relationships assigned or required in workplaces.

Sponsors

Sponsoring relationships involve a more senior and influential person in an organization can advocate for their mentee, help that person network and connect with others, improve their chances for advancement, or suggest positions for them to other colleagues (De Welde & Stepnick, 2015; Murphy et al., 2017). The sponsorship itself is suggesting that the sponsee is ready for the position, the job, the honor, etc. As noted earlier, historically, men have been much more likely to reap the benefits of sponsorships than women, however, as the interview data uncovers, the women in this study benefited greatly from sponsoring relationships.

Peers

Peer relationships are relationships between equal colleagues at a similar career stage, who are of similar work status, who may work on the same team. These colleagues support one another, share information, problem-solve, and provide feedback and friendship (Bland et al., 2009; Murphy et al., 2017). These associations tend to be highly *relational* and built on a foundation of mutual *trust*.

Executive Coaches

Executive coaching relationships provide opportunities for self-reflection, establishing career goals, feedback, opportunities for guided practice in new behaviors or development or improvement of a specific skill set (Murphy et al., 2017).

Learning Partners

Learning partner relationships are from within the woman's network of friends, family, or personal network who are able to learn together. These partners often supply needed support and validation from external sources. Their perspectives may aid in decision-making or problem-solving (Murphy et al., 2017).

Relational Mentors

Relational mentoring may provide women additional opportunities for growth. Relational mentoring focuses on mutual growth and development, empathetic and authentic connection, and draws from relational-cultural theory (RCT) which situates one person's goals and development in connection with others (Jordan, 2018). Each person in the relational mentorship gains something from the mutuality of the relationship (Gammel et al., 2017). This relationship model is different from traditional mentorship; the relationship is absent the power dynamic. Both parties have wisdom and expertise brought into the relationship, and it is sought and valued by both participants. Growth goals do not have to be the same, and in the relationship connection, both exhibit growth. For example, the LEAD group discussed so much in previous chapters began as a peer relational mentoring group. There was a spontaneity in the mentoring of the interactions within the group, deepening as the group members grew to know each other better, learning about the skills and talents each woman had to offer.

Interview Participants

Five women who have served in or are presently serving in leadership positions at Lesley University have contributed their thoughts about mentoring and being mentored in their careers. These are women with ties to Lesley University who have been mentored, are acting as mentors, and those who have been both mentored by and are mentoring other women.

Dr. Lisa Ijiri, Vice Provost for Assessment and Accreditation (Academic Affairs and the Accreditation Liaison Officer), has been a member of the Lesley community since 2012. She is a Fulbright scholar and a seasoned academic administrator with extensive international program experience. Previously, she worked for nearly two decades at Curry College in Milton, MA, both in leading the Program for Advancement of Learning (the country's first college support program for students with learning disabilities) and as an Associate Dean.

Professor Emerita Anne Larkin was a professor in the Graduate School of Education and co-leader of the Lesley/Kennedy/Longfellow Partnership: Integrating Technology into the Curriculum. From 1991 to 2008, she served as the director of the Cambridge Chapter of Say Yes to Education, Inc., a non-profit scholarship program established in collaboration with the Weiss Foundation, Lesley University, and the Cambridge Public Schools. She founded and served as the first president of Personal Advocacy and Lifetime Support (PALS), Inc., an organization that helps families plan for the future of their children with disabilities.

Margaret McKenna is President Emerita of Lesley University, having led Lesley for 22 years and driving its growth from 2,000 to 10,000 students. As a civil rights attorney, she served as deputy counsel in the White House and as undersecretary of the US Department of Education under President Jimmy Carter. She led the transition teams for President Bill Clinton, Boston Mayor Thomas Menino, and Massachusetts Governor Deval Patrick, and was President of Suffolk University in Boston. She has served on the boards of many health, education, and charitable organizations and is currently chair of the Boston Human Rights Commission.

Vivian Poey, Professor in Photography and Integrated Studies, is a faculty member in Lesley's College of Art and Design and a recipient of the Massachusetts Art Education Higher-Educator of the Year Award. Before joining Lesley, she was a mentor in a photography apprenticeship program for high school students at the Manchester Craftsmen's Guild and was an artist in residence in the Pittsburgh Public High Schools. She then became an artist teacher at the Children's Studio Public Charter School for the Arts and Architecture in Washington D.C. She has taken on leadership positions at Lesley: Program Director of the Art, Community and Education M.Ed. Program; most recently as the co-chair, and now, the chair of Faculty Assembly.

Sandra Walker is Interim Dean of the Graduate School of Arts and Social Sciences (GSASS), graduate programs that prepare agents of social change to bring bold new thinking to their fields. Before becoming Interim Dean, she served as the Associate Dean of GSASS. She brings over 30 years of higher education experience to this role that included positions at Harvard University, Babson College, and Massachusetts General Hospital. In this current role, her oversight of the school includes initiating short- and long-term goals, managing the administrative leadership of the school, and administering cross-university collaboration, along with implementing all facets of the university's strategic plan that relate to the school.

The following are vignettes relating to types of mentoring relationships as illustrations of the six types of mentoring relationships explained previously.

Mentoring

Few of the interviewed women actually had formal assigned mentoring or had been part of a planned or institution-based mentorship. All had informal mentors, some who reached out on their own (as opposed to being part of a formal mentoring program), as in the cases of Lisa, Anne, and Sandra, and some interviewees connected with people from whom they learned their jobs and learned about academia, as with Margaret and Vivian. All of our interviewees connected with people who saw leadership potential in them and found a way to encourage growth and development. The theme of *connection* with a person who saw possibility and served as a guide, or a lighthouse (Pemberton, 2021) was evident in all these excerpts.

Anne considered that she had had two key mentors, Dean Lenore Parker and Dean June Fox. Dr. Parker recruited Anne to work at the LAB School, with a small group of 8 students, and, after seeing her success in the classroom, asked her to be part of the undergraduate Lesley faculty.

> Lenore was the one who started my whole career. . . . She mentored me through that whole process. . . . She had confidence in me, and I knew that. And the second mentor was June Fox, who was to me not only a dean but a close friend. June was someone who wanted to learn all about you, what your family is like and you can share with me any problems. I'm here for you. And she did that the entire time that I was there. And she just was one of these people, if anyone was a mentor, she was. Those were the two key mentors, and there were others. . . . Some of my colleagues, they knew I was new to the college, and they were just terrific. I just wanted to fit in, but I wanted to have my voice about what teaching was all about. . . . They were also mentors to me. If I had a problem, I was not embarrassed to ask them questions and they were very sweet all along the way. And then I found they were asking me more often [for my ideas].

Lisa, too, did not have the benefit of a formal mentoring program but shared how she benefited from advice and networking opportunities. "I've certainly had many informal mentors. I've also had many lateral and direct supervisors . . . from whom I've learned a great deal. But I've never been at an organization, where they formalized the mentorship role in a way that was experienced by the whole organization or by my unit." . . . A woman (at her former college) who was dean at the time "took me under her wing. That was as close to a formal mentor as I could get . . . She even said to me, 'Look, I'm going to mentor you. You're going to be a college president if you want to'. . . we both parted from Curry before I had the chance to take full advantage of that relationship, but I never found somebody [else] in that sense, who said to me, 'You know you could go far. I want to meet with you and make sure you get the things that you need to go farther.'" Here again, *trust* was a major factor in this informal mentoring relationship: her colleague's trust that Lisa had the drive and abilities to advance, and Lisa's trust in her colleague which allowed her to accept her coaching and guidance. She mentioned that another colleague suggested that she join the Professional and Organizational (POD) Network which was beneficial to her career. Lisa also commented that, "I think that were it not for some of what I learned from others, and what I was guided towards, I would not have advanced to where I am now."

When Vivian first came to Lesley, Arlene Dallalfar "approached me about joining the New England Center for Inclusive Teaching Fellowship group. You know that she was finding people from each school and so she asked me if I would join, and I think that really became the beginning of my informal mentorship." Vivian believes that the mentoring she has received has led to her success at Lesley. "(without) all of those people that I have collaborated with, I don't think I would have been doing much. I would have been doing a lot of service; I don't think I would have ever published much or done a lot of work that would have gotten me to a full Professor."

Sandra grew up understanding mentoring; she was an athlete at the national level in Trinidad-Tobago before she came to the United States. She had a coach who chose her for the netball team (an all-girls sport). . ."Even back then, I had mentors in my life. I always grew up in this type of woman empowerment zone who always tuned me into the things that I needed back then. "When I started working, I had mentors . . . I have chosen people to align myself with, and rely on them for guidance, for conversation." Sandra also mentioned that Julia Halevy was one of her mentors at Lesley and they still keep in touch, as she does with many people who have been informal mentors to her. Sandra's mentors "contributed to my growth and development . . . and these mentors were able to steer me on the right path with the decisions I had to make back then." When she was working at Harvard Medical School in the cardiovascular lab as support staff, "the woman who ran the lab saw something in me, some promise, something. And she said you have to go back to school, that's the only way you can climb the ladder. She was so instrumental in my life and I really did go back to school . . . I did really truly appreciate her."

Sponsorship

Anne related her story of being sponsored by Lesley President Margaret McKenna to be the director of a scholarship program (Say Yes to Education). "She called me in to say, 'Anne, I have got a grant for you that you can't refuse '. . . Then she told me about Say Yes . . . I said, Margaret, I'm very happy with what I'm doing . . . I am very busy! And so she said, 'Think about it.' Then I went home and talked to Tom (her husband) and he said it sounds very exciting . . . And I thought, what an opportunity to work with these kids and really make sure they make it. That's why Margaret is another mentor because she believed in me. She could have offered it to anybody. And she said, 'I knew this was something that you would love to do!'"

Peer Relationships

The theme of collaboration also ran through all the interviews. There were many comments about learning from peer colleagues among the women interviewed. These leaders valued what they learned from their peers and also felt that their peers gained from the collaboration.

Vivian related her positive feelings about the women who have collaborated with her at Lesley: "I think that my mentors have really been my collaborators. I realized that almost all the work that I've done and starting the development of the whole ESL arts program was a collaboration. . . . so I have learned a lot by collaborating with others, I mean the people that I've had to work with closely on anything. . . . I don't know that they would describe themselves as mentors necessarily; . . . I would because I feel like I learned a lot. That's where I've gotten my entire foundation. . . . I think that I've mentored the way that I was mentored, which was not formal but just sort of collaborating and helping and having other people's backs." So, to Vivian, her mentorship at Lesley was actually a series of *collaborations* with fellow faculty members offering each other information, guidance and support.

Anne, too, believed that her leadership skills developed from working with her peers.

> The teachers, the faculty were great. I just felt that everybody at Lesley was on my side. The key was that I did do outreach to faculty from other divisions and from other schools. I started at the undergrad (school), got to know all of them, and then when Dick Wylie (Dr. Richard Wylie, former dean and vice president of Lesley College) started the graduate school, and then he asked me to come up to the graduate school and that's when I met all of these amazing people. I was just very fortunate that I had the opportunity to be around people that really wanted to share, that really wanted to contribute, and that really wanted everyone to succeed. I think it made me feel stronger, that I stopped having doubts about what I didn't know and what I did know because I learned a lot!. . . I learned from them, I learned from the readings I did, I learned from everybody because they were good models.

Margaret: Margaret and former Chancellor Sherry Penny, of the University of Massachusetts, Boston, formed a group of the women university presidents in Massachusetts together.

> And every time a new woman came, we invited her. Mentoring each other, really . . . as we felt it was a really high trust group. It was a place where we could bring problems and talk in a safe space and it was terrific. Because one of the things with being a university president is there is nobody to talk to. You can't really talk up and you can't really talk down. If you're lucky, you have somebody inside and outside, which I had, [that] you can talk to, but it's a difficult position to be in. So we had each other. . . . At times there were three of us, at times there were eight of us. It was a great support system and a mentoring system, and we were mentoring to each other.

Executive Coaching Relationships

Many of the participants believed that mentoring or coaching has made a difference in their careers and feel that it's important to make a contribution to the careers of others.

Margaret: "Now in this part of my life that I've got a lot of experience and I have some skills and I've learned a lot of things. Sometimes the hard way. And I have a responsibility to share them."

Sandra: "We think we're giving so much to these folks but in reality, we're gaining so much from them, the insights, just the way they think, and they are opening their eyes to new things. I've totally gained so much from them and it's also a way of giving back as others are navigating their own paths."

Lisa: "Even if it's just to take the call from somebody who is referred to me who's thinking about getting into admissions work for the first time . . . I think it's always really clarifying when you have those kind of career questions conversations. and someone early in their career is hungry for that guidance."

Learning Partner Relationships

Anne and Tom Larkin are a good example of a strong learning partner relationship. Together, they founded PALS (Personal Advocacy and Lifetime Support, Inc.), an organization that helps families plan for the future of their children with disabilities. (It is now part of ARC.) When talking about being advocates for their own adult son with a disability, and their hopes for other parents, Anne said,

> You have to fight, it wasn't easy. That's why we started PALS. I wanted people to know that parents can do a lot. You have to know the laws, you have to know the rules, you have to know people, you have to know all your politicians. . . . I was determined that these kids would have a chance.

Their partnership has accomplished good work in Massachusetts and beyond for many years!

Relational Mentoring

Sandra commented on her relational outlook on mentoring:

> It's really a two-way dialogue . . . I don't want to enter a relationship where I feel that I am giving all the time. I want it to always be back and forth, back and forth. So that the person also feels comfortable that they're bringing

> something to the table, that it's not just me coming all the time to give advice and make suggestions. But they can also say, "I'm thinking about this, and what do you think?", and they are bringing their own ideas to the frame of the conversation.

I asked Anne specifically about mentoring Barbara Ulm and Jose Ribero in the Say Yes to Education Scholarship Program as their close relationship was always visible to the people observing their work together. "Barbara and Jose were the most amazing people as far as staff . . . I always say that Jose was the heart of the program. We worked as a team; and it really was a team. We shared everything. I respected both of them for all their knowledge . . . . My team and I ran our own ship, and we did things that others didn't contemplate!. . . With Say Yes, having a team like Barbara and Jose to me meant it all. Barbara took care of everything." They accomplished so much together and, as this first Say Yes program was so successful, I remarked to Anne that she probably mentored George Weiss so that he could replicate the program elsewhere, which he did! Anne remarked, "He said, 'You are a model for us' and that was lovely to hear."

Vivian recounted,

> mentorship is based on trust, and so I think you need to develop that trust before you become a mentor. I don't think it's an obstacle to have either an assigned mentor or a mentor that you just (develop). . . I need that relationship and I guess it's not that you can't develop it, but you can't assume that because somebody has somehow been set up as a mentor that that's going to function in real life. I have a handful of students that contact me every you know, year, a couple years for advice about schools, about work, about career. . . One just invited me to a wedding. . . . It's nice, you know. It feels good to be tapped on a regular basis.

Emerging Themes Across Conversations

There were common themes across all the interviews. None of the women interviewed had been involved in an institutional mentoring program, but all had learned from more experienced individuals or peers and colleagues. All believed that mentoring had made a difference in their leadership skills. Some sought out colleagues, as Margaret did when she became President of Lesley; some were approached by others, as Vivian experienced when she first came to Lesley. Some were sponsored, as Anne experienced when Margaret suggested that she become the director of the Say Yes to Education scholarship program. All suggested ways to find mentors, as Lisa did when she joined the POD Network or as Sandra did when she explained that she learns from so many of her professional relationships and that she continues to keep in touch with her mentors to this day.

Common themes also included stories of relational mentoring, the need for trust in relationships, the way that collaboration on projects brings mentoring and learning benefits to all collaborators, and a great appreciation for the many mentors that appeared in these leaders' lives. Each of the women interviewed expressed the idea of giving back and the benefits of being open to opportunity.

Margaret's story of how she came to run Jimmy Carter's campaign in Rhode Island is an example of being open to opportunity:

> I ran his campaign in Rhode Island, and I got that because a friend of mine was from Georgia and she said to me one day, "Do you want to meet Jimmy Carter, he's running for president." I said, who's Jimmy Carter and she said, "Come over on Sunday." And I said, I'm playing tennis. She said, "Just come over." So I came over. I [had] just played tennis, I was all sweaty and yucky. And that's how I met him. . . . And so I left my job and joined the campaign and was the state director in Rhode Island. There were four women in the whole country who were running states, and we ran "girl states", as we called them, baby states, North Dakota, Rhode Island, you know, little states. That was the first time, in 1976, women were allowed to run states. It changed quickly after that. That was Mary King. And that's how I got involved in the Carter Campaign, at a meeting at her house on Capitol Hill. She thought of me.

Strategies to Increase Opportunities for Mentorship

Ideas for mentorship approaches arose from the interviews and research conducted for this chapter. These include different forms of outreach, formal mentoring programs sponsored by institutions, affinity groups, and writing groups.

Outreach

Many of the women leaders interviewed had stories of choosing people to help them, asking questions of more experienced colleagues or university leaders, reaching out to others, joining organizations or projects, founding organizations if one did not exist, and staying in touch with mentors and people mentored. All these things mattered. Creating and maintaining relationships and seeing potential for growth in connecting with others were also running themes in the interviews.

Formal Mentoring Programs

Lisa supported formalized mentoring systems,

> I'm wholeheartedly in support of formalized mentoring structures and systems. That includes those outside of your institution program, so you're

> exposed to cohorts and also within institution programs, I think, are terrific and I absolutely wish we had had something like what Lesley is doing [now]. In my career as a faculty member, I think it would have been tremendously valuable for me at that time. Likewise, I think there's still a gap in chair development; I think that that's true at a lot of universities still. Moving forward I think there's stronger networks and structures for mentoring of faculty in the role as faculty and that even doctoral training programs are building those in . . . So, I think I wouldn't take it as a given that there's sufficient structure and support for women to advance to the different leadership levels. You can just look at the distribution of leadership roles in higher education and see that they're still far to go for that, so I think the first way that mentoring could achieve a positive outcome is to help with equalizing of opportunity and representation; I think there's still a lot of work there that needs to happen.

Informal Affinity Groups

Sandra mentioned the value of the meetings of BIPOC faculty and staff several times a year at Lesley to catch up with each other, learn more about what others were doing across the university, and see themselves in the others within a majority white institution. Meetings like these can also function as informal mentoring opportunities. Margaret founded several groups to help support women in their leadership development.

Writing Groups

Cassese and Holman (2018) proposed writing groups as models for peer mentorship among female faculty in political science as an approach to increase research productivity. Penney et al. (2015) explored a faculty writing group based on a relational model of interaction. These writing groups serve several purposes: to provide peer mentoring (particularly in a field with few women); to support women's research; and to improve the rate of promotion and tenure among women faculty. Vivian spoke about writing an article with a colleague so that they would both add to their academic writing experience. This book was created through a subset of our original LEAD group, and we met, in person and virtually, to write together and critique each other's writing as we developed our chapters over time.

All these collaborations helped colleagues develop important skills and negotiate new institutions or positions, accomplish research projects, and supported leadership development.

Interview Guide

Initial questions and prompts are listed. Follow-up comments: Can you tell me more about that? How so?

I'd like to explore your ideas about mentoring or being mentored in higher education. For this conversation I define mentoring as a purposeful relationship, and formal mentors as either assigned to you or chosen by you for a specific purpose.

1. Have you had a formal mentor?

   Yes: Record and go to #2. . .
   No: Ask/record: Why was it that you did not have a mentor?

   How might you have benefitted from having a mentor?
   How did you fill the gaps and build skills?
   Go to #4

2. Have you chosen your own mentors to help you develop?
3. How did mentoring contribute to the development of your leadership skills?
4. How have these experiences shaped your views on mentoring?
5. Have you mentored others either formally or informally in higher education?

   - Do you feel that mentoring others has made a contribution to your own career? How so?
   - Earlier you mentioned ______ as a pitfall or an obstacle. Could you share a bit about that?
     OR
   - In your experience, were there any obstacles to overcome in mentoring? What did you learn from these obstacles?

6. Do you believe that mentoring has helped you achieve success in your career? How so?
7. Given what you've learned, and what I've learned from you, could you see any ways that mentoring could help other women achieve leadership positions in higher education?

References

AAUP Update. (2020). Data snapshot: Full-time women faculty and faculty of color. *American Association of University Professors 12/9/2020.* https://www.aaup.org/news/data-snapshot-full-time-women-faculty-and-faculty-color

Bierema, L. L. (2017). No woman left behind: Critical leadership development to build gender consciousness and transform organizations. In S. R. Madsen (Ed.), *Handbook on research on gender and leadership*. Edward Edgar Publishing.

Bland, C. J., Taylor, A. L., Shollen, S. L., Weber-Main, A. M., & Mulcahy, P. A. (2009). *Faculty success through mentoring: A guide for mentors, mentees, and leaders*. Rowman & Littlefield Publishers, Inc.

Cassese, E. C., & Holman, M. R. (2018). Writing groups as models for peer mentorship among female faculty in political science. *PS: Political Science &Politics*, *51*(2), 401–405.

De Welde, K., & Stepnick, A. (2015). *Disrupting the culture of silence: Confronting gender inequality and making change in higher education.* Stylus Publishing, LLC.

Gammel, J. A., Motulsky, S. L., & Rutstein-Riley, A. (2017). Relational mentoring: Connection, mutuality, and empowerment. In A. B. Knox, et al. (Eds.), *Mapping the field of adult and continuing Education: An international compendium*. Stylus Publishing, LLC.

Jordan, J. V. (2018). Evaluation. In *Relational – Cultural therapy* (2nd ed., pp. 77–94). American Psychological Association.

Keohane, N. O. (2014). Leadership out front and behind the scenes: Young women's ambitions for leadership today. In K. A. Longman & S. R. Madsen (Eds.), *Women and leadership in higher education*. IAP-Information Age Publishing.

Meschitti, V., & Smith, H. L. (2017). Does mentoring make a difference for women academics? Evidence from the literature and a guide for future research. *Journal of Research in Gender Studies*, *7*(1), 166–199.

Murphy, W. M., Gibson, K. R., & Kram, K. E. (2017). Advancing women through developmental relationships. In S. R. Madsen (Ed.), *Handbook on research on gender and leadership*. Edward Edgar Publishing.

Pemberton, S. (2021). *The lighthouse effect: How ordinary people can have an extraordinary impact in the world*. Zondervan.

Penney, S., Young, G., Badenhorst, C., Goodnough, K., Hesson, J., Joy, R., McLeod, H., Pickett, S., Stordy, M., Vaandering, D., & Pelech, S. (2015). Faculty writing groups: A support for women balancing family and career on the academic tightrope. *Canadian Journal of Higher Education*, *45*(4), 457–479.

Seltzer, R. (2015). *The coach's guide for women professors who want a successful career and a well-balanced life*. Stylus Publishing, LLC.

White, J. S. (2014). HERS at 50: Curriculum and connections for empowering the next generation of women leaders in higher education. In K. A. Longman & S. R. Madsen (Eds.), *Women and leadership in higher education*. IAP-Information Age Publishing.

6 Leadership Identity Development

Can the Voices of Diverse Women Be Heard?

Gail Simpson Cahill and Stephanie A. Spadorcia

Introduction

The articulation of the LEAD model began with a literature review of leadership theories. We posited that an understanding of past models would help us shape our unique model of leadership development. What we quickly unearthed is that the field of leadership theory is vast and continually growing. Our literature review of leadership articles identified 66 published theories since 2000 (Dinh et al., 2014). We discovered that leadership theories were often compartmentalized in disparate and fragmented ways and historically have focused on the leader, per se, and not the follower or the context (Glynn & Raffaelli, 2010). It also became evident that the term leadership has been synonymous with men, and therefore the voices of women, in general, have been muffled if heard at all, and the voices of BIPOC women were practically nonexistent.

An extensive analysis of empirical and theoretical articles that contained three or more references to leadership theories identified six focal leadership constructs (Meuser et al., 2016). These perspectives are (a) charismatic leadership, (b) transformational leadership, (c) strategic leadership, (d) shared leadership, (e) trait approaches to leadership, and (f) leadership and diversity. Despite the growing research in the field, leadership studies in higher education have not grown in proportion and, in fact, are considered to be under-researched (Angawi, 2012).

We decided to begin with a summary of these six most frequently identified leadership constructs in order to critique what exists in the literature and then provide a framework for what the LEAD framework contributes. Then, we morphed into contemporary leadership development practices in line with relational feminist perspective development. We drew a comparison between two competing perspectives: (1) "traditional" hierarchical leadership training with the adage "add women and stir"; and (2) an evolving perspective that draws upon feminist theory to emphasize relational leadership development to promote leadership identity development. We identified distinctive competencies deemed to be important for current leaders that were uncovered in the literature search

DOI: 10.4324/9781003057208-6

with a lens toward the development of women in higher education. Finally, we conclude the chapter with a description of a LEAD group activity that resulted in a visual creation that represented the vision of the LEAD group at the end of its first year of work together.

Focal Leadership Constructs

Charismatic Leadership

Max Weber coined the term, charismatic, to describe leaders who gain power and authority based on personal appeal and charm (Auerbach, 2013). Today, charismatic leadership is often referenced as a "neo" charismatic leadership model to describe the advancement of Max Weber's model to its new uses in private organizations. Neo-charismatic leadership is a style of leadership that is positively associated with a sensitivity to people's emotions, the development of a vision, and influencing change, in particular, in a crisis situation; in contrast, it is negatively associated with an overreliance on the leader, a misarticulation of goals, and overall poor management (Jamal & Baker, 2017). A charismatic leader, therefore, may not be able to transfer the leadership to other members of a team, thereby thwarting the maintenance of substantive changes to an initiative or organization. The LEAD model incorporates charismatic leadership in that it is a model which is sensitive to individual emotions; however, it does not rely on a leader to build a vision or goals but rather has adopted the feminist principles of shared and transparent power to co-construct these items (and others) with its membership.

Transformational Leadership

Transformational leadership theory was coined by James MacGregor Burns (1978 as cited in Caldwell et al., 2012) and is a leadership model that integrates social values and individual purpose to develop a mutually desirable future (Caldwell et al., 2012). Transformational leadership acknowledges the reciprocity between a leader and followers and challenges both to analyze their assumptions and develop new solutions (Caldwell et al., 2012). According to transformational leadership theory, a leader is a positive role model who inspires and motivates followers by challenging them to be innovative and creative, while demonstrating genuine concern for the individual needs and feelings of each follower. Transformational leadership theory is often cited as providing the underpinnings of the nature of leadership with a clear focus on social values and individual purpose. Some drawbacks of this theory include the possibility that followers might show blind trust and be led by an autocratic leader and the concern that this type of leadership might not work in a crisis or overly complex situation (Lee, 2014). The LEAD framework incorporates transformational leadership's focus on individual and institutional values to develop ongoing solutions using a collaborative relational approach.

Strategic Leadership

Strategic leadership involves the leadership of top management to learn, remain flexible, anticipate, and work with others to initiate change (Boal & Hooijberg, 2000). Strategic leadership is posited as the most integrative form of leadership, given the complexities of generating strategic designs within often uncertain organizational environments (Avolio & Gardner, 2005). Strategic leaders work to ensure that appropriate action steps are undertaken at critical times. They link the present context of an organization with the long-term future. Connections among leadership teams and followership are also often missing from this theory (Boal & Hooijberg, 2000). The founders of the LEAD framework strategized with members to initiate individual and organizational change to augment the "faces" of women in leadership roles. Unlike strategic leadership theory, the LEAD framework emphasized collaboration among members and built strong relationships to center its collective work.

Shared Leadership

Shared leadership is a group process that implies a relational interplay between ever-changing events and processes (Wood & Dibben, 2015). It is a distributed leadership style that exercises group members' mutual influence toward achieving individual, group, and organizational goals. Shared leadership supports the continuation of how a group works, even after members of the group leave and others join. It is an emerging view of leadership and as such the empirical research supporting this approach is limited (Serban & Roberts, 2016). A few recent findings, however, support its effectiveness. For example, Choi et al. (2017) demonstrated that shared leadership improved a team's organizing and planning effectiveness. The LEAD group incorporated many shared leadership tenets. The group constructed norms together and then began each meeting with a review and/or discussion of them. Using a shared leadership lens, the group co-constructed each agenda and worked to ensure that all voices, regardless of roles, were heard and valued. All LEADers also shared responsibility to ensure that agenda items were met. Through rotating facilitation of meetings members were supported in leading agenda items and acting as a mentor to others.

Trait Theory Leadership

Trait theory is a leadership approach that attempts to define human personality in terms of traits, or patterns of behaving, that predispose an individual to successful leadership. Trait theory has a long, yet spotted history. Considered one of the first approaches to leadership, it appears early in the literature (e.g., Gordon Allport, Raymond Cattell, Hans Eysenck) until Stogdill's influential review concluded the research had failed to produce a clear list of consistent traits that predict leadership effectiveness (Stogdill, 1948). More recently, however, researchers have a renewed interest in leadership traits (Lucas & Caspers, 2014) and emotional intelligence (Pekaar et al., 2018) due in large part to advancement in more sophisticated personality assessments and meta-analytic research tools (Dinh et al., 2014). Currently, it appears that trait theory is positioned for integration with other emerging theories. The LEAD group did not focus on individual traits, per se, but rather the relationships built from and because of individual traits from the multiple intersectional identities of members; in essence, LEAD became the collective relational collaboration of all members.

Leadership and Diversity

The globalization of organizations has diversified the demographics of the workforce. It has also shed light on the underrepresentation of women in leadership roles. For example, according to a recent survey, only 16.9% of Fortune 500 organizations are led by women leaders, and less than 3.2% of women of color hold executive board seats (Catalyst, 2013 as cited in Meuser et al., 2016). In another study conducted by the University of Colorado Denver Women's College (2013), *Benchmarking Women Leadership in Higher Education*, the "higher the fewer" paradigm was highlighted – where the higher the rank and leadership positions are in higher education, the fewer women there are in those positions. This is juxtaposed against the fact that women have earned more than 50% of earned doctorates since 2006 (Fowler, 2019; University of Colorado Denver Women's College, 2013). What does this say about the leadership development opportunities for women in higher education if more than 50% of earned doctorates come from women yet only a fraction of college presidents are women? The *Asilomar Declaration and Call to Action (Declaration)* (Madsen & Rosser-Mims, 2015) not only put an urgent call to action for organizations to be a catalyst for change in the perception of women as leaders, but also to develop a plan to augment more women leaders worldwide. Perhaps the best way to describe the research and current practices in the leadership development of women, is disjointed, limited, and ripe for further research (Meuser et al., 2016). Therefore, this has led us to ask – *How do the dominant theories of leadership development support diverse women's LEADership development? How can a LEAD model contribute to "doing power differently"?*

Doing Power Differently

We were inspired by the *Omega Institute's Women's Leadership Center* (https://www.eomega.org/omega-womens-leadership-center) catch phrase

#doingpowerdifferently. This embodies what the LEAD framework aims to ask – how can leadership development not only change the members of the group but also open more opportunities for the diversity of perspectives and identities at an institution? In turn, will that influence the evolution of an institution? We posit that initiatives focused on leadership development for women should try to change the macro perspective (van Esch et al., 2017) of leadership development. We have concluded that the way leadership development has operated for years is not the way to be more inclusive and allow more voices at the table. This is especially important in the current context of higher education where access to education and ensuring diverse voices across the gender spectrum are at the decision-making tables. Therefore, a development focus that comes to the work from a feminist relationship perspective is not just about having more self-identified women at the leadership table but strives to make sure there is more diversity of perspectives at the leadership table for all in the institution. It makes space for the recognition of the impact of different identities that women hold in their own leadership development and ultimately leadership identity formation.

The origins of feminist praxis highlighted the power differential based on assumptions of gender identity and how this significantly impacts how members are perceived and work as leaders (Thompson, 2002). Kumra (2017) points out the drawbacks of a liberal feminist approach to leadership development where just equal access and treatment will result in more women in leadership development opportunities. Kumra goes on to point out that despite systematic efforts to minimize the inequalities in leadership development opportunities, it has not fixed the numbers: Women are still outnumbered by men in leadership positions across fields and sectors. The LEAD model moves leadership development forward more by saying development efforts should be built towards an intersectional feminist approach – recognizing how power plays out at the intersection of gender, race, and other identities. There is an opportunity for macro-level change by recognizing the different perspectives coming from the intersections of individual identities: race, gender identity, sexuality, disability status, and/or cultural and religious identities.

Relationship to Other Leadership Theories

Leadership development from the traditional models highlighted earlier assumes that women have to take on the dispositions, stances, perspectives, and ways of operating where the central thesis is *What I am is not going to work or is not enough.* That thesis denies the strengths that an intersectional feminist perspective would bring to a development model. A feminist perspective will support leadership identity development of members over the long term and ultimately impact institutional change for more leadership development of community members. The historical stance perpetuates the notion that there is a privileged set of competencies that I, as a deficient woman, need to possess before taking on leadership positions and help facilitate leadership for others. We see that described in the charismatic and trait model of leadership development. Women continually operate against the assumption of lack of fit (Hoyt & Simon, 2017), which is a deficit-model driven framework. In contrast, an intersectional feminist perspective assumes there are strengths that come from the recognition of diverse identities and examining the role that power plays in different contexts for those intersections.

This book documents what happens when self-identified women faculty collaborate on a leadership development model that centers the different identities of individual members as they enter leadership roles, which ultimately impacts their leadership identity development. More importantly, it documents how a model attempted to impact change and make macro-level changes in an organization using the understandings learned from different identities as a strength to their own leadership identity development (The Asilomar declaration and call to action as compiled by Madsen & Rosser-Mims, 2015).

Missing Components of These Models

Storberg-Walker and Natt och Dag (2018) assert that accepting other traditional models as the ideal to work towards and ascribe to, diminishes the role of the discovery and imagination to explore frameworks that will allow for new understandings of leadership expression, identity, and growth for individuals. We saw that in our review of the six leadership theories discussed earlier, so many of the traditional models emphasized the leader, the vision, characteristics, and decision-making of the individual person, not the relational nature of leadership and what could be learned mutually from each other in the development experience. One member of our group started with a goal to learn all the things that will make her a "great leader" as a set of items to check off on a list. During the evolution of her leadership identity in the group, there was a moment of recognition that the apex of leadership development is not to meet an ideal but to create space with others to work on their own leadership development in the context of the challenges they faced together in their individual roles.

The LEAD group worked in a space that utilized a feminist praxis where relational theory principles allowed members to move beyond traditional accepted ways of doing things and know-how. Together, the group instead used creativity to create a model that responded to the context and uncertainty of the institution and the landscape of higher education at that time (Storberg-Walker & Natt och Dag, 2018).

As the landscape of higher education changes and societal movements are rightfully demanding more inclusivity and opportunities, the traditional models of leadership development described earlier will continue to perpetuate a one-dimensional leadership paradigm. In those models, it is the premise that institutions just need more women to be in leadership to make change. The adage of "add women and stir" is one that many no longer accept. Instead, what is needed is new leadership development models that operate from a feminist relational and intersectionality stance. This creates development that fits the context of the institution and contexts in which they are operating at that time – therefore, it will not be the same from one institution to the next but rather will be different based on the context of the institution. The uncertain times in higher education in this decade demand that this work be done to survive and respond to the needs of the students to make a macro change as an institution. As the *Asilomar Declaration and Call to Action* (compiled by Madsen & Rosser-Mims, 2015) outlined, it is imperative that individual women work to be agents of change and empower others to support leadership development. A feminist relational group process approach to leadership development supports self-mentoring as a tool for the empowerment of the individual and creates networks within an organization for this to occur.

It seems to me that whereas power usually means power-over, the power of some person or group over some other person or group, it is possible to develop the conception of power-with, a jointly developed power, a co-active not a coercive power (Bierema, 2017, p. 150).

We posit that Leadership Development, especially for self-identified women in a higher education setting, should try to change the macro perspective (van Esch et al., 2017) of leadership identity development. The way in which leadership development has centered and privileged skill-based development derived from a single perspective has resulted in less inclusivity. It has prevented more voices from being at the table, particularly in providing access to higher education. In order to ensure that diverse voices are at the decision-making tables, feminist relational leadership development is not just about more women at the leadership table, but it is also about the diversity of the identities of the various perspectives at the leadership table and examining how power interplays at those intersections.

Leadership development programs that focus only on gender will not make the necessary changes in an institution. A sole focus on gender as the only differing factor will result in more of the same, and the current criticism of what is considered antiquated models of feminism where white middle-aged women in a colonial perspective continue to dominate (Grande, 2003). This will not create more inclusive leadership frameworks or make space for people at the table (Ngunjiri & Gardiner, 2017) but instead perpetuate the myth that all women's issues are the same based on the sole identity of gender alone.

We see the irony of this as ultimately the LEAD model developed from a homogenous group of women faculty with similar identities. We recognize that what we have found useful for leadership identity development may not be the same for other members of our institution or at other institutions in different contexts with varying identities. But rather, we assert that the LEAD framework, which is feminist in approach and embodies relational ideals for working together, would support other groups and settings to be creative to develop other frameworks. The framework would allow varying identities to make space for development in a supportive way to encourage the leadership identity development of its members.

Leadership Development as an Act of Social Justice

Models of leadership development that are feminist and relational in nature will allow more individuals to step up into leadership within an institution. This evolved model of leadership development allows a group to define leadership more dynamically and express it in multiple dimensions that are more likely to be accepted in the institution they come from and affect change at multiple levels – not only from the top down. Traditional models of leadership development often result in a culture where those who point out the problems in the organization model are vilified and then in turn are not put into positions of leadership to make changes (Bierema, 2017). An institution that has its mission to promote social justice, such as a university, has to adjust models of leadership development to minimize this ostracizing of individuals by assuming similarities based on single identities only such as gender, for example, all women in leadership are the same.

Storberg-Walker and Natt och Dag (2018) assert that privileging models that prioritize logic and cognition over other types of knowledge sources such as those described in the seminal work of Belenky et al. (1986) limit the full leadership development for self-identified women based on the dynamic ways learning occurs in a feminist relational paradigm. It diminishes the future of the field and the further development of potential frameworks. We assert that the LEAD framework will impact leadership development for members and will change the macro perspective (van Esch et al., 2017) of leadership development over time.

This can be a strange understanding for some members coming into a leadership development space. Self-identified women with other identities that intersect with marginalized groups often come into leadership development opportunities thinking they need to take on and learn the dominant skills to be successful. Women operate against the assumption of lack of fit (Hoyt & Simon, 2017) – therefore, they approach leadership development from a deficit model. Instead, we suggest that a feminist relational approach will emerge more naturally and support institutional change to advance social justice over time. In turn, more leaders from diverse backgrounds and identities will emerge. The Leadership & Community Engagement Program (L&CE) at the University of Texas at El Paso (Nuñez-Mchiri & Chacón Silva, in press) operates under a similar framework. This program focuses on women's leadership development of Latinx members of the community at the border – bringing to light how women are working to take leadership in their community to address relevant issues to women and children.

How to Ensure Diverse Women's Voices Are Heard

Leadership Identity Development: The LEAD Framework

Effective leadership development programs recognize how dynamic a construct of leadership development is. Models of development should be constructed to allow for shifts in the power differential in an institution to respond to changing times and contexts. Ultimately, the goal of leadership development should be to allow individuals to change the macro perspective (Storberg-Walker & Natt och Dag, 2018). We assert that the following elements need to be present in leadership development frameworks that operate from a feminist relational perspective.

Creativity

Creating a self-mentoring group within a setting that responds to the individuals and contexts within the setting is key. There needs to be recognition that no one leadership development framework will fit all institutions. It needs to be robust and co-constructed as group membership changes and challenges faced by the institution change as well. Leadership identity development should be centered in the model.

Social Identity

Leadership development models need to hold a place to recognize the various social identities members hold and how they shift in different contexts. All individuals hold various identities across social and personal realms. The "Social Identity Wheel Activity" (e.g., Equitable Teaching, University of Michigan) recognizes key identities individuals hold in social interactions that impact their own perception of themselves and how others perceive them in various situations. They include gender, sexual orientation, ethnicity, race, nation of origin, physical and emotional disability, first language learning status, socio-economic status and class, religious affiliation, tribal or indigenous affiliations, and body size/type. Each identity and intersection of identities will hold different power and perceptions depending on context, model of leadership development, and conditions within an organization or institution.

Adult-Learning Theory

A relational feminist framework of leadership development needs to be grounded in adult learning theory (Knowles, 1968; Rachel, 2002). Adult learning theory is rooted in self-directed learning where the learner directs their learning – asking questions, actively involved in inquiry about their own development. Leadership identity development that uses adult learning models will bridge the gap between the difference in knowing leadership development theory and supporting individuals' leadership identity development (Bierema, 2017). Ultimately minimizing inequities (Bierema, 2017) and ultimately impacting the institution in which the group is operating.

Feminist Praxis

A leadership development model that aims to support progress for members of an organization needs to engage in a feminist praxis. Feminist praxis is defined as putting feminist theory into action (Evans & Chamberlain, 2015). This action of praxis can be a tool to directly address issues that face members who are impacted by contexts where power and privilege minimize their leadership identity. Chapter 3 highlighted the societal barriers that impact women's leadership development. It is widely recognized in the literature that the balance of family and childcare with working in a career often falls on the mother or self-identified women in the majority of family structures – therefore, recognizing this barrier and working to dismantle the hurdles within an institution would not only support self-identified women who face this challenge but also widen opportunities for other members of the institution that also balance work and family care needs. That is only one example of a barrier. There are multiple examples of such barriers present in all organizations. Therefore, feminist praxis widens the lens through which a leadership development framework could support more diverse individuals to engage in development and ultimately make room for more to join the table.

Gender Consciousness Training

Gender consciousness training leads to increased levels of confidence and ambition in both men and women, resulting in more equality not only for self-identified women but also for other identities including race and ethnicity (Drury & Kaiser, 2014; Harnois, 2016). Recent work in this area highlights that an intersectionality approach to conceptualizing gendered consciousness has a positive impact on self-identified men's advocacy in this area (Harnois, 2016). Gender consciousness training impacts ways in which groups collaborate and work together including making agendas, assigning responsibilities for tasks, and even taking up talking space and yielding the floor for more voices to speak on issues (Hutchinson & Mann, 2004). Bierema's work (2003, 2005, 2017) highlights the need for organizations to understand the gendered power relations within a system. This work highlights that when gender consciousness training is not considered part of development opportunities individuals act in a state of gender unconsciousness and, therefore, there is no action towards change. When willingness and awareness are not matched, self-identified women in leadership positions themselves do not act on needed changes to remove barriers to leadership opportunities. In order to address sexism directly to expand the capacity in all leaders, gender consciousness needs to be built within all members of an organization.

Mentoring

Mentoring is crucial to any leadership development model – otherwise, it is a training that is static and not practiced. It is important for a feminist relational model of leadership development (Gammel et al., 2017) that individual members mentor each other and create networks of mentors outside of the group and institution. Chapter 5 in this volume explores the role that mentoring plays in individual self-identified women's leadership development.

Context

A key component to leadership development should be the recognition that context matters about the individual and where they are situated in various contexts. Identity factors such as gender and race are viewed differently based on the context at the time and change the power differential depending on the circumstances. Hoyt and Simon (2017) point out that women tend to shift their leadership style depending on the context and perceived audience. For instance, in more male-dominated situations, women tend to be more directive and top-down as compared to contexts in which there is more diversity, particularly of gender, women lead in a more relational style. The LEAD framework described in this book draws from the contexts in which developing self-identified leaders are working within different contexts and examines how power and perceived power vary.

Conclusion

Leadership development needs to prioritize leadership identity development for individuals in an institution. Although this book is focused on leadership development for women, it highlights the need for a feminist relational framework of leadership development for all members of a community across gender identities, races, ethnicities, and sexual orientations, as well as professional or discipline-based identities. When models that are driven by deficit analysis, skill-based, or "add women (or any other descriptors of diversity) and stir" are used in leadership development initiatives, the opportunity to advance the leadership identities of members is missed, and ultimately negatively impacts the mission of the institution. Thus, the results are less impactful and short-lived. In an institution of higher education, this results in less capacity to respond to a more diverse, global society in a manner that pushes real change and social justice.

References

Angawi, G. T. (2012). Neo-charismatic leadership: A new theory for effective leadership in higher education. *Educate*, *12*(2), 34.

Avolio, B., & Gardner, W. L. (2005). Authentic leadership development: Getting to the root of positive forms of leadership. *The Leadership Quarterly*, *16*, 315–338.

Belenky, M. F., Clinchy, B. M., Goldberger, N. R., & Tarule, J. M. (1986). *Women's ways of knowing: The development of self, voice, and mind.* Basic Books.

Bierema, L. L (2003). The role of gender consciousness in challenging patriarchy. *International Journal of Lifelong Education*, *22*(1), 3–12.

Bierema, L. L. (2005). Women executives' concerns related to implementing and sustaining a women's network in a corporate context. *Organization Development Journal*, *23*(2), 8–20.

Bierema, L. L. (2017). No woman left behind: Critical leadership development to build gender consciousness and transform organizations. In S. Madsen (Ed.), *Handbook on research on gender and leadership*. Elger.

Boal, K. B., & Hooijberg, R. (2000). Article: Strategic leadership research: Moving on. *The Leadership Quarterly*, *11* (Yearly Review of Leadership), 515–549. https://doi.org/10.1016/S1048-9843(00)00057-6

Caldwell, C., Dixon, R., Floyd, L. A., Chaudoin, J, Post, J., & Cheokas, G. (2012). Transformative leadership: Achieving unparalleled excellence. *Journal of Business Ethics*, *109*(2), 175–187. https://doi.org/10.1007/s10551-011-1116-2

Choi, S., Kim, K. & Kang, S. (2017). Effects of transformational and shared leadership styles on employees' perception of team effectiveness. *Social Behavior & Personality: An International Journal*, *45*(3), 377–386. https://doi.org/10.2224/sbp.5805

Dinh, J. E., Lord, R. G., Gardner, W., Meuser, J. D., Liden, R. C., & Hu, J. (2014). Leadership theory and research in the new millennium: Current theoretical trends and changing perspectives. *The Leadership Quarterly*, *25*, 36–62.

Drury, B. J., & Kaiser, C. R. (2014). Allies against sexism: The role of men in confronting sexism. *Journal of Social Issues*, *70*, 637–652.

Equitable Teaching. (n.d.). *Social identity wheel* [Webpage]. University of Michigan. https://sites.lsa.umich.edu/equitable-teaching/social-identity-wheel/

Evans, E. & Chamberlain, P. (2015). Critical waves: Exploring feminist identity, discourse and praxis in Western Feminism. *Social Movement Studies*, *14*(4), 396–409.

Fowler, C. (2019). *Nevertheless, she persists: Women leadership in higher education.* (Electronic Thesis or Dissertation). https://etd.ohiolink.edu/

Gammel, J. A., Motulsky, S. L., & Rutstein-Riley, A. (2017). Relational mentoring: Connection, mutuality, and empowerment. In *Mapping the field of adult and continuing education.* Routledge.

Glynn, M., & Raffaelli, R. (2010). Uncovering mechanisms of theory development in an academic field: Lessons from leadership research. *The Academy of Management Annals*, *4*, 359–401.

Grande, S. (2003). Whitestream feminism and the colonist project: A review of contemporary feminist pedagogy and praxis. *Educational Theory*, *53*(3), 329–346.

Harnois, C. E. (2016). Intersectional masculinities and gendered political consciousness: How do race, ethnicity and sexuality shape men's awareness of gender inequality and support for gender activism? *Sex Roles*, *77*, 141–154.

Hoyt, C. L, & Simon, S (2017). Social psychological approaches to women and leadership theory. In S. Madsen (Ed.), *Handbook on research on gender and leadership*. Elger.

Hutchinson, J. R., & Mann, H. S. (2004). Feminist praxis: Administering for a multicultural, multigendered public. *Administrative Theory &Praxis*, *26*(1), 79–95.

Jamal, J., & Baker, H. (2017). The mediating role of charismatic leadership communication in a crisis: A Malaysian example, *International Journal of Business Communication, 54*(4), 369–393. https://doi.org/10.1177/2329488415572782
Knowles, M. S. (1968). Andragogy [sic], not pedagogy. *Adult Leadership, 16*, 350–352, 386.
Kumra, S. (2017). Reflections on glass: Second wave feminist theorizing. In S. Madsen (Ed.), *Handbook on research on gender and leadership*. Elger.
Lee, M. (2014). Transformational leadership: Is it time for a recall? *International Journal of Management and Applied Research, 1*(1), 17–29. https://doi.org/10.18646/2056.11.14-002
Lucas, M., & Caspers, S. (2014). Leadership and adult development: Towards a unified neuro-psycho-economic approach. *Behavioral Development Bulletin, 19*(4), 83–90. https://doi.org/10.1037/h0101084
Madsen, S. R., & Rosser-Mims, D. (Compilers). (2015). Asilomar declaration and call to action on women and leadership. *Women and Leadership Affinity Group, International Leadership Association.* http://www.ila-net.orgCommunities/AG/Asilomar_Declaration2015.pdf
Meuser, J., Gardner, W., Dinh, J., Hu, J., Liden, R., & Lord, R. (2016). A network analysis of leadership theory: The infancy of integration. *Journal of Management, 42*(5), 1374–1403. https://doi.org/10.1177/0149206316647099
Ngunjiri, F. W., & Gardiner, R. A. (2017). Future strategies for developing women as leaders. S. Madsen (Ed.), *Handbook on research on gender and leadership*. Elger.
Nuñez-Mchiri, G. G., & Chacón Silva, A. (in press). Towards a new leadership and community engagement model for Latinas transfronterizas. *Frontiers, 42*(3).
Pekaar, K., Bakker, A., Born, M., & van der Linden, D. (2018). The consequences of self- and other-focused emotional intelligence: Not all sunshine and roses. *Journal of Occupational Health Psychology*, https://doi.org/10.1037/ocp0000134
Rachel, J. R. (2002). Andragogy's detectives: A critique of the present and a proposal for the future. *Adult Education Quarterly, 52*(3), 210–227.
Serban, A., & Roberts, A. J. B. (2016). Exploring antecedents and outcomes of shared leadership in a creative context: A mixed-methods approach. *Leadership Quarterly, 27*(2), 181–199. https://doi.org/10.1016/j.leaqua.2016.01.009
Stogdill, R. (1948). Personal factors associated with leadership: A survey of the literature. *The Journal of Psychology, 25*(1), 35–71. https://doi.org/10.1080/00223980.1948.9917362
Storberg-Walker, J., & Natt och Dag, K. (2018) Creativity in theorizing for women and leadership: A multi-paradigm perspective. In S. Madsen (Ed.), *Handbook on research on gender and leadership*. Elger.
Thompson, B. (2002). Multiracial feminism: Recasting the chronology of second wave feminism. *Feminist Studies, 28*(2), 337–360. https://doi.org/10.2307/3178747
University of Colorado Denver Women's College. (2013). *Benchmarking women's leadership in the United States*. University of Denver.
van Esch, C., Assylkham, K., & Bilimoria, D. (2017) Using organization and management science theories to understand women and leadership. In S. Madsen (Ed.), *Handbook on research on gender and leadership*. Elger.
Women's Leadership Center. (2021, January 22). https://www.eomega.org/omega-womens-leadership-center
Wood, M., & Dibben, M. (2015). Leadership as relational process. *Process Studies, 44*(1), 24–47. http://ezproxyles.flo.org/login?url=https://search.ebscohost.com/login.aspx?direct=true&db=aph&AN=109454765&site=eds-live&scope=site

7 The Girlhood Project

A Relational Exploration of Learning, Leading, and Becoming

Amy Rutstein-Riley

In 2008, I was asked by a colleague to develop a short workshop for girls in the Cambridge, Massachusetts, area on any topic of my choosing. The request came in response to the need for more youth development programming for girls in the Cambridge Public Schools. At the time, I was teaching a women's studies course and taught a unit that focused on body image, critical media literacy, and identity. This curriculum was a very popular theme of the course and one that I knew would translate well into programming for early adolescents and adolescent girls. I created a three-week workshop and trained my college students to facilitate the workshop with the youth participants. Titled *Girls, Media, and You,* developed in partnership with the youth serving organization Tutoring Plus of Cambridge, Massachusetts, and initially funded with grant support from the Massachusetts Campus Compact Coalition, it became the seed for *The Girlhood Project (TGP) https://www.thegirlhoodproject.org/*.

Since 2008, TGP had grown into a robust academic-community based partnership offered at Lesley University and served preadolescent and adolescent self-identifying girls from a range of greater Boston communities. Participants were recruited from public and private school partnerships, area community centers, and by word of mouth. TGP ran for nine weeks each spring semester from 2008 to 2022, with over 300 girls and 350+ college, graduate, and doctoral students participating in the program. College-community partnerships were becoming chic in the early 2000s and funding to support TGP was available. What started out as a small program grew in size, scope, purpose, and impact.

At its essence, TGP is a relational learning community guided by feminist group processes and a belief in the power of relationships to foster the development of voice, self-knowledge, identity, and competencies of confidence and self-authorship. Central core principles of TGP include: (1) the belief that participants are agentic and capable of contributing new knowledge to the understandings of girls' and women's development and to leading change in their individual lives, families, schools, and community contexts, and (2) girls and women are powerful and not problems to be fixed, as much of the public discourse might suggest. Over the life of TGP, the essence of the program and its principles

DOI: 10.4324/9781003057208-7

strengthened as its delivery from year-to-year became shaped by the experiences of its many participants. Processes of co-construction, critical reflective practice, and a commitment to teaching and learning in relationship guided my own leadership approach and the ways I worked with youth and university students who participated in the program.

A starting place for my work with TGP's participants was the commitment to co-creation of the learning community. Power typically held by authority, (professor, university) would be shared with the participants – the girls and university students – with the professor, assuming a guide-by-side facilitator role. I mentored, coached and supported a team of teaching assistants, research assistants, and doctoral fellows who had themselves previously participated in TGP, and who contributed to the construction of the program's pedagogy, content, and design. Built into the program design was the idea that participants could repeat participation in the program for multiple years of middle school and high school, with high school participants assuming greater responsibility for mentorship of their younger peers. The focus and thematic areas of programming were constituted anew each year. Changes were based upon the collective interests of the participants and organized around several central TGP themes (see Figure 7.1,

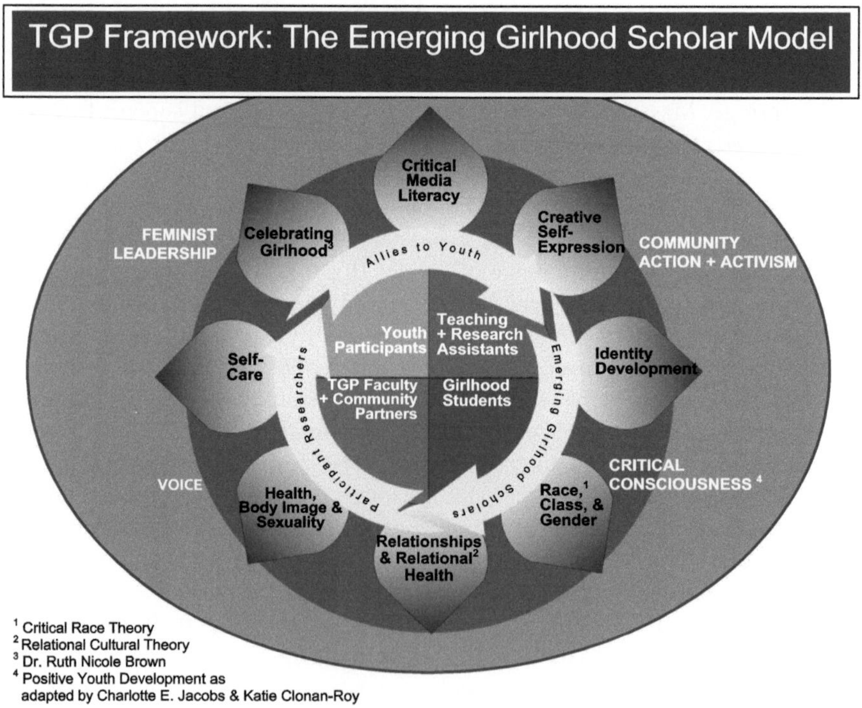

Figure 7.1 The TGP Framework: The Emerging Girlhood Scholar Model.

The TGP Framework: The Emerging Girlhood Scholar Model). This offered ongoing developmental opportunities for repeated participants.

TGP's repetition model and benefits were also true for the university participants. College students would participate in the course, *Girlhood, Identity, and Girl Culture*, the academic arm of TGP, and upon completion of the course could apply in subsequent years to serve as teaching and research assistants, project managers, program operations support (IT, website, fundraising), with opportunities for graduate interns and doctoral teaching fellows. This *Emerging Girlhood Scholar Model* reflects the flow of whole person development – academic, social, and emotional – that transpired for the participants in the program, including myself, the professor/founding director.

Each spring, TGP collaborates with several Greater Boston area community partners to invite middle and high school-age girls to Lesley's campus to participate in nine weeks of girls' groups that are co-facilitated by Lesley University students. Together, girls and university students explore how social and cultural constructions of girlhood – sexuality/ies, race, class, ethnicity, education, the media, and current events – impact their lives. TGP utilizes disruptive feminist pedagogy, feminist group process, and critical media literacy to center girls' experiences and construct new knowledge about their lives (Rutstein-Riley & Ziergiebel, 2018, 2020) while fostering the development of feminist leadership, voice, critical consciousness, and community action and activism among all learning community participants (Clonan-Roy et al., 2016; Rutstein-Riley & Ziergiebel, 2018, 2020; Weiner et al., 2020).

Long before I developed TGP or co-developed LEAD with two of my colleagues, I had studied relational-cultural theory (RCT), and integrated it into my approach to teaching, learning, leading and research (Miller, 1996; Jordan, 2010, 2018). And long before I studied RCT, I held strong beliefs in the power of relationship and connection to facilitate growth, and that growth has the potential to be multidirectional and growth fostering for all participants in the relationship. When I studied RCT, I found a language for the practices that I believed were important for and instrumental to women's growth and development (Gammel et al., 2017). In 2000, I participated in a year-long feminist group process training with Cambridge Family Institute in Watertown, Massachusetts. This group created the space to explore the impact of centering women's gender, shared power in practice, collaborative decision-making, and the development of voice. This immersive experience transformed my views of teaching and learning and changed the way I engaged with students and colleagues. It provided the spark that fueled my move toward engaging with power differently and reformulated my understanding of teaching and learning as a relational act with the potential to change my students, myself, and my community. This experience and my shift in self-understanding framed the grounding themes and design of TGP, and in turn the LEAD group that followed.

TGP's Pedagogical Approach

Grounded in the belief that girls are the experts of their own experience, TGP resists cultural narratives that position girlhood as a universal experience or as an at-risk gender category that needs to be fixed. We affirm that knowledge is socially constructed by historical, cultural and political contexts. We work with self-identified pre-adolescent and adolescent girls using media (music, print, digital) as an entryway to deconstruct and reconstruct knowledge about girlhood. We believe that relationships and building a caring learning community are essential to working with girls. We honor and celebrate girlhood in all its forms.

In the *Girlhood, Identity, and Girl Culture* course (the academic arm of TGP), university students are provided with a theoretical introduction to the field of girls' studies that is informed by Relational Cultural Theory, Critical Race Theory, Positive Youth Development, feminist pedagogy, critical media literacy, and intersectional understandings of girls' and women's identity development (Brown, 2009; Clonan-Roy et al., 2016; Daniels & Zurbriggen, 2016; Delgado & Stefancic, 2001; Jordan, 2010; Lerner et al., 2005; McArthur, 2015; Rutstein-Riley & Ziergiebel, 2018, 2020). We build on these theoretical foundations with experiential programming that engages intersectional identity development and multimodal expression as tools for socio-cultural critical analysis. *Girlhood* students engage in feminist praxis, equipped with the TGP Toolkit of experiential, dialogue-based, and arts-infused activities, to co-facilitate their girls' groups.

In preparation for facilitation of TGP, the university students complete a rigorous academic preparation integrating the exploration of girls' studies scholarship

Box 7.1 The TGP Toolkit.

Essential components of the TGP Toolkit include:

- Community norming
- Feminist group process
- Critical deconstruction and production of new media
- Identity mapping
- Journaling and arts-based activities
- Music and dance
- Critical discussion
- Narrative and storytelling
- Celebration

with theory on girls' and young women's identity development (biopsychosocial, cultural, social identities) and how social institutions influence and contribute to the construction of girls' and women's identity development, that is, family, school, religion, and community. The intersection of theory and practice informs and reinforces the development of relationship, trust, vulnerability, and group formation as facilitation techniques are studied, practiced, and refined. Relationship-building and feminist group process minimize power differences between faculty and university students, thus centering students' individual and collective knowledges, developing expert voice, and emerging leadership, in turn activating the capacities of the university students to facilitate the nine-week girls' group sessions at the heart of TGP (Rutstein-Riley et al., 2013; Rutstein-Riley & Ziergiebel, 2018, 2020). While power remains visible within the context of TGP, we rely on feminist process to acknowledge it and dismantle it through our shared work.

Prior to the start of the nine-week girls' groups, experiential learning sessions held with the university students enliven the feminist group process, providing a space to experience, reflect and integrate new knowledge as they collaboratively design and co-construct new ways to explore the lived experiences of the girls and young women participating in TGP. In tandem with experiential sessions, is the active engagement of reflective practice through dialogue in large and small groups, just-in-time critical reflection of learning through the use of Critical Incident Questionnaires (adapted from Stephen Brookfield's CIQ instrument, Brookfield, 1995), and post TGP whole group reflection sessions. Key to the potential for transformation and development of new ways of seeing and knowing self and others is the ongoing critical reflection on the integration of theory and practice, providing the seeds for TGP Emerging Scholars to develop. What has evolved over the years, as revealed in data collected over the life of TGP, is the opportunity for participants to develop greater self-awareness and self-understanding, greater understanding of others, and the development of voice to be used to advance the individual and collective interests of TGP participants both within the TGP space and beyond the walls of the university into the communities they live – school, family, places of worship, work, and social relationships.

During the nine weeks of girls' groups, all participants join in the co-construction of weekly content, activities to center exploration, and engage in reflective research practices on the collective experience. Youth and university students alike partake in participatory action research methods to understand self, other(s), community, and the ways in which TGP influenced growth and transformation. Some of these approaches have already been described, with significant opportunities for data collection with the university students – reflective journals and assignments, CIQs, dialogue groups, and other artifacts. In addition, the girls participated in data collection through journaling, artistic expression, creation of Photovoice projects, development of digital and video content, production of zines, and engagement in dialogue to capture reflection upon experience in the moment.

Each source of data helped me and the TGP team to understand the impact of this experience, to refine the model, and to be highly responsive to the desires of the participants. Pivoting and responding to critical incidents in the group was necessary for centering the girls as drivers of this experience, while balancing this with support and safety within the group. The TGP Framework evolved over time, enhanced by the contributions of its participants, and strengthened through a dynamic exchange with girlhood scholars in the field. This reflexive collaborative stance produced a highly active, sometimes chaotic, relational learning community that centered a range of diverse voices of the girls in partnership with the university students. Narratives of their lives were amplified through the context of feminist leadership, critical consciousness, and community action and activism. Concepts and program themes of identity development; race, class, and gender; creative self-exploration; critical media literacy; celebrating girlhood; self-care; health, body-image, and sexuality; and relationships and relational health identified in the TGP Framework provided the weekly substance interrogated in and through relationships developed among the girls and the university students. Each weekly session of each year of the program, the girls and university students, together, in allyship, focus on the thematic areas most relevant to the girls' groups in the current moment, and they, together, direct how they choose to interrogate, deconstruct, and reconstruct the issues of greatest salience.

TGP's Core Values

TGP and the Emerging Girlhood Scholar Model have been influenced by several key ideas in feminist discourse which show up in TGP's co-constructed core values.

Power Is Shared

In the design and delivery of TGP, a decision was made to disrupt traditional power dynamics such as those the girls experience many of their school days with teacher as authority and with power held by adults and other authority figures. The practice of feminist leadership maintains a commitment to the stance of power-with rather than power-over. Sharing power, distributing it, and intentionally holding a stance of power-with is disruptive and empowering for those who get to engage with power differently. While feminist leadership deliberately works to subvert the dominant hierarchical power structure it also requires feminist leaders to proactively reconstruct and rename shared power Determining how to best share power through collaborative and collective means necessitates inviting others to be a part of making and sustaining change as a model for ethical engagement (Dugan, 2017; Shea & Renn, 2017; Christensen, 2013; Lazzari

Box 7.2 TGP's Co-Constructed Core Values.

- Power is shared.
- Girls are experts of their own experience.
- Connection and mutuality in relationship is growth fostering.
- Girls and women are allies.
- We do not fix.
- We bring our whole selves or as much as we desire.
- We are a safe space; safe ≠ comfortable; we work with tension and productive discomfort.
- There is no universal Girl or Girlhood.
- Knowledge is socially constructed; we deconstruct and reconstruct our own in relationship.
- Identity is complex, multilayered, and intersectional.
- Disorientation leads to transformation.
- We practice shared vulnerability (Hill, 2016).
- We practice unlearning (Brown, 2009).

et al., 2009; Owen, 2020). This value is core to the design of TGP and one that requires consistent commitment and program norms to ensure.

Centering Girls and Women – Girls Are Experts of Their Own Experience

TGP holds primary that girls and women are experts of their own lives. In TGP, we position girls and women at the center of the relational learning community, and it is through honoring and creating space for the participants to bring to voice their interests, wants, and desires that growth and transformation are possible. There is no predetermined curriculum or established learning outcomes or objectives. Knowledge is not held by a single expert. Rather, through building relationship and trust, inviting vulnerability, and creating the space for leadership to flourish, girls and university students together become the leaders of this experience (Denner et al., 2005; Edell et al., 2013; Rutstein-Riley & Ziergiebel, 2018). Partnerships, mentorships, and deep relationships can develop between girls and women in which guidance, not instruction, creates women-girl partnerships. However, in TGP, the benefits of partnerships, mentorships, and deep relationships are multidirectional, so that all participants regardless of age or status, experience the potential for growth and change. TGP embodies the belief that feminist leadership thrives when supportive relationships, whether peer-to-peer or peer-to-adult, are created and supported (Bond et al., 2000; Denner et al., 2005; Girl Scout Research Institute, 2008).

Relational Connection and Allyship

The participants in TGP spend significant time building connections. We intentionally utilize a range of activities from the TGP Toolbox to establish an inclusive space where flourishing is not only possible but encouraged. Attending to the range of diverse social identities present in the TGP space we cultivate a stance of allyship, navigating the complexities of identity work by supporting exploration and self-expression. Girls and university students together become allies as they learn about self and others over the course of nine weeks of girls' groups. TGP is a *come as you are in whatever aspect of self you would like to share* type of space. The safety to do this is made possible by intentionally building relational connections with allies showing up each week ready to engage from that standpoint.

Creating Space for Authenticity and Voice

Part of effective feminist leadership and pedagogy is creating supportive environments where progressive transformation can happen (Christensen, 2013; Girl Scout Research Institute, 2008; Lewis, 1993; Owen, 2020). Denner et al. states, "creating a place to be authentic does not mean encouraging everyone to say whatever comes to her mind. It means helping girls know, state, and act on what is most important to them" (2005, p. 95). In TGP voice is both physical speech as well as its absence. Voice is movement with or without speech. Voice is also an external representation of the internal self. In TGP we invite all aspects of voice and encourage it in all of its manifestations to take up space and to make space for others. Through this focus on voice participants come to articulate what matters most to them and is where co construction of authentic leadership in community occurs (Owen, 2020). In TGP, creating safe or safer space is always paramount, with co-constructing a brave space (Arao & Clemens, 2013) as an aspirational goal.

Feminist Pedagogy and Praxis: Deconstructing and Co-Constructing Knowledge

Feminist pedagogy is a collaborative educational method that shares power and authority between teachers and students, privileges inclusion of students' authentic knowledge, respects interpersonal relations, and makes connections between academic study and the world outside the classroom by using experience as a resource (Hooks, 1994; McCusker, 2017; Perrier & Withers, 2016; Shrewsbury, 1997; Walker, 2007). It does not sound revolutionary, but rather good teaching, however, it is in fact revolutionary and emancipatory.

The formation of the relationship between teachers and students is perhaps the most foundational element to feminist pedagogy. Approaching the development and delivery of TGP with feminist pedagogy at its core allows me to create at the outset a teaching-learning partnership with my students, one that centers all participants as knowledge producers. Sharing power in the classroom dismantles the traditional power-over hierarchies by creating a space in which students and professors are equal contributors to the learning process (Webb et al., 2002) while reorienting learning from an individually oriented goal to one of co-constructed and collective as all members of the course, individuals as students and teachers work to achieve mutual goals (McCusker, 2017; Minnich, 2005). Professors move beyond the role of expert and become learners alongside their students (Hammer & Giordano, 2001; Welde et al., 2013). Simultaneously privileging individual and collective relational voice as a way of knowing, by engaging in critical expression and agency, encourages students to express their views as they develop confidence in themselves and their abilities (Maher & Tetreault, 1994; Stake & Hoffmann, 2000). Students become "empowered knowledge-producers" rather than "passive knowledge-consumers" (Chow et al., 2003, p. 260).

Students gain deeper respect for the diversity of personal experience, remaining focused on the interconnectedness of people as co-producers of knowledge by sharing thoughts and experience with others (Webb et al., 2002). Feminist pedagogy supports learners to push past their comfort zones and sit with tension and disorientation as a pathway to challenging one's deeply held beliefs and values (Pereira, 2012; Shah & Kopko, 2016; Mezirow, 1990). These moments of discomfort invite students to reexamine their own perceptions, the bases of those perceptions, and the power embedded in existing knowledge creation (Boler, 1999; Linkon, 1992; Mezirow & Associates, 1990).

In preparation for facilitation of TGP's girls' groups, university students collaborated with me (the professor), classroom peers, and a teaching and research assistant team to come together as a learning community, to co construct new knowledge about themselves, others, and the scholarship of the field. Newly envisioned norms about teaching and learning shift and open up space for individual, collective, and community-based learning, with all learners capable in turn multiplying the learning experience and its individual and collective impacts.

Leading for Change – Self and Community

TGP is a feminist project with an agenda for moving change from the individual to the learning community to beyond the walls of the university to the communities in which our emerging girlhood scholars live and thrive. Feminist leadership prioritizes social change and feminist leaders are change agents. Each year, as the final weeks of TGP come into focus, an end-of-year TGP celebration is planned. The event is planned with the youth at the center, a celebration of girlhood. It is a luxurious celebration honoring the girls and university students, marking moments of resilience, growth, and change, and sharing the many ways participants used creative expression to narrate their diverse experiences in TGP.

Food, music, art, and dance take over and topped off with gifts of love, college swag, and lots of Instagram-ready photos.

However, as a project of feminist leadership, individual exploration and growth as well as communal transformation is not the only potential outcome, but how girls and university students in turn bring their learnings, transformed views, and new ideas for change into their communities. Over the years we have witnessed feminist clubs being formed, fundraising initiatives for local politicians serving their communities, creative installations in their communities, and perhaps the most important impacts being felt in their own homes where girls enter into new discussions with family members about issues never before approached.

Learning About TGP's Impact

A final core value of TGP is an ongoing focus on critical reflection. Each year of the program I would submit a new Institutional Review Board for Human Subjects application so the TGP leadership team (professor, TAs, RAs, graduate assistants and doctoral fellows) in partnership with the youth and university students could reflect upon and make meaning of the impact of this project on all its participants. Diverse research methods, including participatory approaches, individual and group interviews, CIQs, and document review techniques were used to assess the experience of TGP participants. The overarching exploratory question guiding the research was: *What is the impact of The Girlhood Project on its participants*? This broad question was followed by many more specific guiding questions, yet what I most wondered about was the impact on the participants in all the small and big ways in regard to their growth and change in the program. This very open research question is the one that has guided my exploration of this program since 2008. Reams of data sets and digital images of artifacts clutter my office and hard drives, and in 2020, in collaboration with my doctoral student Sarah Doyle, we undertook a small study (included at the end of this chapter) with a group of our Lesley University graduates who had completed TGP, to look back on their experience. We were truly curious about the impact of participation on where they landed after university, and how, if at all, TGP informed their future selves, and if TGP impacted the ways in which they think about the concept of feminist leadership, in particular. Close to 150 surveys were sent out via email (for a substantial group of past students, we lacked email contact information), though a significant number bounced back. Using our social media presence, we were able to reach out to additional participants, and for the purpose of this chapter, we will share what we learned from this particular group of TGP university student participants.

Experiencing Feminist Leadership in TGP

Participants reported that engagement in the TGP group process method fostered their understanding of the concept of feminist leadership and facilitated their confidence in how to enact it. By actively dismantling and sharing power in the TGP space, the participants became active learners and drivers of their own development, directing their own experience and feeling empowered to do so. Once they moved outside of the university setting, the participants applied what they had learned about feminist leadership to their developing careers, volunteer opportunities, and further education.

Several survey respondents wrote about their feelings of validation and empowerment during their TGP experience as they navigated through the changing power structures. The participants remarked that "no one's thoughts were dismissed as 'wrong' or unimportant" because in the TGP setting, "no one was to hold absolute authority above the rest"; TGP "flips patriarchal power structures on its head by engaging in the collective learning." The intentional sharing of power creates a sense of equal footing among TGP participants. One participant noted that the sharing of power "reminded me that everyone's voices and experience is important, no matter their age, no matter their experience in life."

This reminder served the students well when creating and leading the Girls' Groups. A strong theme in the survey data spoke to the TGP core value of centering girls and women. The university students placed the girls' experiences at the center, focusing on topics that the girls identified as important. Strategies for sharing power and centering girls was a new learning for most of the university students, and survey responses point to the tension in doing so; many wished to truly co construct the experience with the youth participants while the actuality of doing so was a very new concept in practice. Respondents described sharing power as "giving a chance for us students to lead the focus groups and designing our girls' weekly agenda"; "actively and consistently listening to the girls"; and "ask[ing] girls for their input." One participant wrote that it was "hard to learn to let go of control, to see that a carefully planned activity wasn't working and deciding to change it in real time. But feminist leadership means taking that ego hit because it's more important to engage the girls in a way that's helpful to them, to the collective group, regardless of your own personal feelings."

By modeling feminist leadership, the TGP Leadership Team encourages the university students to be active participants in the group process, to collaboratively engage with each other, while placing the girls at the center of the experience. "TGP introduced me to feminist pedagogy. Before that, I had no idea I was capable of leading or learning in a way that made me feel smart, that valued my ideas and contributions." With intention, the leadership team strove to model and create enough safety for participants to share power and to foster an inclusive space where all participants' voices were welcomed, demonstrating the shift in structure from top-down power to distributing power through a strengths-based approach, thereby fostering the development of relationships and partnerships. Partnership, rather than power, drives the success of the Girls' Groups. The act of "leading by example of going through the process of teaching and supporting undergrad students to be mentors and partners to other girls," creates an environment that uplifts the university students while partnering with and centering the girls in their groups.

Defining Feminist Leadership

> *TGP helped me define what feminist leadership was in the first place. It didn't necessarily help inform my definition, it built it. I was able to learn and teach with folks of different backgrounds and experiences and formed ways of working together. It pushed me to recognize my privilege and admit gaps in my knowledge by learning from women who did the same, leaders to me, helping me to become a better feminist myself.*
>
> – TGP survey respondent

A definition of feminist leadership emerged from the responses submitted by the TGP participants. Drawing upon their perceptions of how they experienced their own feminist leadership skill development, the TGP participants offered insights into the definition of what it looked like to be feminist leader. Three themes emerged from the responses: (1) dismantling, or undoing, hierarchical power structures is essential; (2) feminist leadership is inclusive; and (3) feminist leaders engage in critical self-reflection.

Dismantling hierarchical power structures means that one should "diminish hierarchy whenever possible and redistribute your power in order to support everyone involved"; it is "meant to challenge the typical male-dominant leadership style" and it "challenges those unhelpful attributes of power-over leadership." Undoing hierarchical power structures is a multi-faceted and dynamic act and described by respondents as, "acknowledging, dismantling, and pushing back against hierarchies that affect girls and women's lives" "while it "sheds light on the systematic injustice" and requires us to "constantly question institutions and norms." Shifting from hierarchical demonstrations of power to feminist leadership requires the active examination and deconstruction of the application of power by and within dominant societal structures and processes: "believing that women and men have equal rights no matter their cultural background and teaching our children this at any age."

Feminist leadership is inclusive by "creating change and bringing voices to the table." By being inclusive, feminist leadership "listens to all voices and uplifts those who are marginalized," while it "amplifies and includes the voices of those oppressed by patriarchy and white supremacy culture." Feminist leadership also refuses to engage in practices by "further 'othering' of marginalized groups." Through "co-constructing knowledge and space," feminist leadership is also relational, as feminist leaders are "aware of power differentials" and intentionally work to "build community." By being multidimensional, feminist leadership seeks to "consider all aspects and identities."

By "showing up every day as an ally to yourself and all women," requires feminist leaders to actively and authentically engage in critical self-reflection, "accepting criticism and feedback" which is not a simple task. Being open and willing to learn, one respondent wrote that being self-reflective meant she had to "admit gaps in my knowledge by learning from women who did the same," while another reflected that it "forced me to see and come to understand my privilege." Feminist leadership is a process that learns by "evolving, always critiquing itself, and always listening to others."

Feminist Leadership Themes

Reflecting upon their experiences in TGP, the survey respondents shared their thoughts about the development of their feminist leadership skills. The growth of the participants' feminist leadership skills was felt in two areas: (1) one's own leadership skills and (2) the leadership of and with others.

Personal growth of feminist leadership skills "allowed me to recognize my strengths and my ability as a leader." A respondent stated, "I began to trust my voice and believe that what I say matters and I deserve to be heard," while another felt it "empowered me to be myself as a whole person who is complex not just as a woman but a woman with many life experiences." Through personal growth, participants expressed a growing sense of confidence to practice leading with others in varying leadership roles within TGP.

Leadership of and with others requires building one's self-confidence and internalized sense of competence. One respondent reflected on her experience as a feminist leader within the Girls' Groups: "it was important as a woman of color to be able to lead by example and allow myself to truly be myself and give the girls space to be themselves in whatever we were doing." Another respondent writes about working in her college peer group, as well as with the Girls' Groups, as she notes that she "became a more comfortable leader through not only the process of working with my group members, but also through active facilitation of the Girls' Group." Taking the skills that one participant gained from her TGP experience, they write that they are "now a leader at my tech organization, striving for equity and stressing the importance of representation of trans and cis women, queer, and GNC (gender non-conforming) folks in STEM, applying competence and confidence to harness my leadership voice." Practicing feminist leadership also means taking risks and reflecting upon those risks, as a respondent shares "exhibiting leadership in a space where I don't know the girls very well is an area that makes me nervous."

Impact of TGP on Life Outside the University Setting

> *I'm working on adjusting company policies to be more inclusive with a focus on the BIPOC at my organization. I've been brought back to the work I'd done with TGP and how difficult it had been to do this incredibly emotional work. I often reflect on how, almost a decade ago, the girls I worked with feared for the lives of their brothers. How they likely still fear for their lives. I keep them at the forefront of my mind, striving to*

> *do my part to make this world a better, safer place for BIPOC and working to open my org up to where it falls short: getting folks from disenfranchised populations in the door.*
>
> – TGP survey respondent

Outside of the university setting, the respondents articulate having remained connected to their TGP experiences. Seventy-seven percent of respondents claim that their work (both professional and volunteer) relates to their TGP participation. Many survey participants write about themselves as agents of social change and how they developed into this role during their TGP semester or semesters, while others discuss how TGP influenced the direction of their studies as undergraduates or graduate students, or in other continuing education settings.

Across their professions identified by respondents, the TGP participants find that their roles in their work have ties to their TGP roots as feminist leaders. When asked if TGP had any impact on their chosen work or volunteer opportunities, the TGP participants shared a range of responses which are included here to illustrate the numerous ways the TGP experience is carried into participants' next developmental phase post university life. Reflected across responses is the developmental thread of becoming, with statements demonstrating the diversity of growth, self-awareness, confidence, competence, and critical consciousness.

"I am interning with another girlx 'leadership program' in the area this fall."

"I'm currently working on how to bridge work I feel passionate about with the field I'm in to bring change in a historically white cis heteronormative male dominated industry."

"I don't think I would have ended up at this job and becoming a part of this community that's now so important to me if I hadn't had the experience with Girlhood first."

"I worked mostly with females who were survivors of domestic violent relationships. While working with them in the confidence of shelter, I was able to utilize this empowerment model that was learned throughout TGP and I think my work with girls and women was heavily influenced by my work within TGP."

"I currently work as a BCBA providing behavioral therapy services to children on the autism spectrum. I work primarily with low-income families of color. I use my experience with TGP to support these families and inform my programming and interventions, especially when working with BIPOC girls."

"I still mentor girls through venues and support and lift up their voices. Then for work, I work at a non-profit indigenous organization with a grant that focuses on kindergarten readiness for Alaska Native families. TGP has helped me learn how to become part of a community – TGP at the time had Black/Brown middle schoolers and as someone Asian who was also a minority but experienced the world very differently than my middle school counterpart, it was important to listen and understand and not fall into the white savior complex. Working in an indigenous organization where I am coming as an outsider, there are similar skills I practice of listening and learning."

"I work primarily with adolescents. It has informed my clinician practice immensely."

"Working in an industry that is extremely white, male-dominated, I have needed to advocate for women in many ways. I am a member of a non-profit that empowers women in the brewing industry and participate in women-led education at my place of work."

"I was interning at a Title I school in Boston, specifically working with middle school students as I did with TGP."

"I work with young adults and children who have Autism. Most of the children that I work with come from lower income households and are BIPOC. The intersectionality framework that I first learned about in TGP informs much of the work that I do in the mental health field. Similarly to how we dissected the media in class with the sexualization of womxn, I have also been dissecting the media with its inaccurate portrayals and misinformation regarding Autism."

"I was just recently a clinical program director for an eating disorder treatment center. The consumers were primarily adolescent females."

"Focus on more awareness on how girls can impact more for the society and world."

Beyond the work that the respondents do professionally, they bring their dedication to social justice into the world as advocates for and allies to marginalized populations. "I've dedicated my time to showing up for racial justice. TGP got the ball rolling with this," reflects one respondent. Feminist identity formation and the commitment to push back against patriarchal norms is acknowledged by several respondents: "I was just a budding feminist at the time and this class/project really solidified that identity for me. [TGP] helped shift my own view of others as competition – to be partners in this patriarchal world instead and to uplift one another." While another recalls, "I feel that it gave me the building blocks to begin living a more feminist lifestyle. I began to look at and interpret so many things differently because of it." And a third respondent shares that "the skills I learned and the lens I now see the world through are what I now carry with me and apply to everything I do." Lastly, in reflecting on the leadership she brought with her from her TGP experience, one participant writes, "Leadership skills have definitely followed me over the past 10 years," while another respondent shares, "It gave me confidence to be a leader in my field."

Many of the survey respondents share how TGP had influenced their academic decisions in their undergraduate, graduate, or continuing education opportunities. One respondent writes that TGP inspired her "to be a lifelong learner"; another individual shares, "it inspired me to change my major to counseling from English"; and another reflects, "TGP helped me build confidence as a student and scholar." Several TGP participants are pursuing (or have completed) graduate degrees, acknowledging the impact that TGP played in the decision to do so: "I wanted to pursue a master's degree so I could finally be in a position where I could create similar spaces for womxn to come together to share their stories, and to feel heard and seen." Another participant has a goal to "pursue a graduate degree at some point, the focus of which would be on creative writing, and how storytelling (books, literature, media, art) affects the social development and self-perception of the young people who consume them."

The Girlhood Project, by design, is a multifaceted exploration of girls' and women's identity development viewed through a prism of relational teaching, learning, and leading. It is difficult to fully illustrate the many moving parts of the TGP Framework as presented earlier in this chapter. A static visual aid does not capture the dynamic movement and intersections of relationships over time as shaped by who is participating in the space and co-constructing the experience. Meaning making in TGP is fluid, context dependent, and constructed in collaboration and reflected upon individually as well as collectively.

In many ways, TGP has been an aspirational program. Its aspiration is to support the forward growth and transformation of all its participants, a lofty and vulnerable goal. The constantly changing social, cultural, economic, and political landscape was regularly shifting, as did the social priorities and lived realities of the youth and university student participants contributing to the many ways of seeing, experiencing, and making meaning of TGP. This chapter sought to provide a window into TGP, its design, structure, pedagogy, and the transformative feminist and girls' studies scholarship that informed its creation and evolution over time. I chose to share but one way of seeing TGP and thinking about girls' and women's development, and the Emerging Girlhood Scholar. Considering the ways university students articulated their views on feminist leadership as acts of dismantling/undoing, inclusion, reflective practice, and of sharing power, I believe makes visible how they experienced growth in their own understandings of self, other, community, and society.

For me, as a relational teacher, leader, and mentor, TGP is at its essence an enactment of mutuality, care, and connection through which growth for girls and women is hopeful, joyful, and powerful.

TGP Survey, 2020

Purpose

Investigate the impact of participation in The Girlhood Project on Lesley Alumni

Background

In 2008, Dr. Amy Rutstein-Riley developed the initial offering of what is now known as The Girlhood Project (TGP). What was first developed as a "special topics" course has evolved into Girlhood, Identity, and Culture (CSCOL-3820), part of The Girlhood Project. Over the years, the TGP team has learned a lot about the impact of our program on our current students and alumni, especially in the areas of personal, academic, and professional development.

Currently, TGP serves girls in middle and high school from several greater Boston communities. Current community partners include: Cambridge, Somerville, Watertown, and Belmont, with other participants from a variety of additional communities. This year alone, we served over 40 youths. As we grow as a program, we continue to self-reflect and seek to learn more about the impact of the project on college and university students as well as on the girls who join us for girls' groups.

This survey seeks to understand how participation in TGP impacted your personal, academic, and professional development. This is not intended to be a course evaluation. Rather, we seek to learn from you – recent and distant graduates – about the meaning you made of your participation in TGP. We ask you to reflect on your experience and memories of TGP to learn how (if at all), and in what ways, TGP impacted you.

Based on a pilot study, we estimate it will take 10–15 minutes to complete this survey, and longer if you opt to write more.

Questions

If you can recall, when was your initial involvement with TGP?
And when was your last TGP experience?
How did you participate in TGP? (select all that apply)

- As a college student
- As a student enrolled in Women Culture and Society, special projects (CSOCL 2115)
- As a student enrolled in Girlhood, Identity, and Girlhood Culture (CSOCL-3820)
- As a Teaching Assistant
- As a Research Assistant
- As a Project Manager
- As a Graduate or Doctoral Student
- As a Research Fellow
- As part of the TGP Teaching Team
- Other? ________

Why did you choose to participate in TGP?

The course aims to impact students in a variety of areas. You may, or may not, have experienced growth in the areas listed below. Please rate the how important the Girlhood course was to your growth in the following areas (Very important, Important, Moderately Important, Slightly Important, Unimportant):

Leadership skills and identity
Feminist consciousness
Social consciousness (relative to race, social class, sexuality, ability)
Feminist leadership
Relational confidence and competence
Other (please specify)

Please elaborate on an area from above that had the most impact on you.

Please provide an example of your greatest area of growth from your participation in TGP.

Please discuss how your experience in TGP impacted your understanding of the ways in which social institutions shape girls' lives.

How did TGP impact the way you think about leadership?
How would you describe/define feminist leadership?
In your estimation, did TGP inform that definition?

(Yes/No)
If Yes, why?
If No, why?

Is your current professional or volunteer work, in any way, related to your experience in TGP?

(Yes/No)
If Yes, please explain how your experience in TGP has impacted your paid employment and/or volunteer experiences.

Have you pursued further education in either graduate study or other formal programs such as trainings or workshops? If so, did TGP influence your educational choices, and if so, how?

Please add anything else you would like to share that we have not asked.

Closing: Thank you for sharing your reflections on the ways in which TGP impacted your life.

OPTIONAL Demographics question – self-identify race/ethnicity, gender, age, graduation year/expected graduation year

OPTIONAL – insert email link (sdoyle3@lesley.edu) for anyone willing to be in touch for further TGP inquiry

Note: Enormous gratitude to all the 650+ participants in TGP who have contributed to the vitality and longevity of this unique program; your participation made TGP. I am grateful for all the lessons I have learned in collaboration with my students and for how with each passing year they helped me grow as a teacher, learner, mentor, and advocate. For this chapter, I also thank Sarah Doyle for her contributions to sifting through reams of articles and data used to inform the construction of this chapter.

References

Arao, B., & Clemens, K. (2013). From safe spaces to brave spaces: A new way to frame dialogue around diversity and social justice. In L. Landreman (Ed.), *The art of effective facilitation: Reflections from social justice educators* (pp. 135–150). Stylus Publishing.

Boler, M. (1999). *Feeling power: Emotions and education*. Routledge.

Bond, L. A., Belenky, M. F., & Weinstock, J. S. (2000). The listening partners program: An initiative toward feminist community psychology in action. *American Journal of Community Psychology, 28*, 697–730. https://www.researchgate.net/profile/Jacqueline_Weinstock/publication/227288242_The_Listening_Partners_Program_An_Initiative_Toward_Feminist_Community_Psychology_in_Action/links/00b495322e0c4ac472000000/The-Listening-Partners-Program-An-Initiative-Toward-Feminist-Community-Psychology-in-Action.pdf

Brookfield, S. D. (1995). *Becoming a critically reflective teacher*. Jossey-Bass.

Brown, R. N. (2009). *Black girlhood celebration: Toward a hip-hop feminist pedagogy*. Peter Lang.

Chow, E. N. L., Fleck, C., Fan, G. H., Joseph, J., & Lyter, D. M. (2003). Exploring critical feminist pedagogy: Infusing dialogue, participation, and experience in teaching and learning. *Teaching Sociology, 31*, 259–275. http://dx.doi.org/10.2307/3211324

Christensen, M. C. (2013). Using feminist leadership to build a performance-based, peer-education program. *Qualitative Social Work, 12*(3), 254–269. https://doi.org/10.1177/1473325011429022

Clonan-Roy, K., Jacobs, C., & Nakkula, M. (2016). Towards a model of positive youth development specific to girls of color: Perspectives on development, resilience, and empowerment. *Gender Issues, 27*. https://doi.org/10.1007/s12147-016-9156-7

Daniels, E. A., & Zurbriggen, E. L. (2016). The price of sexy: Viewers' perceptions of a sexualized versus a non-sexualized Facebook profile photograph. *Psychology of Popular Media Culture, 5*(1), 2–14.

Delgado, R., & Stefancic, J. (2001). *Critical race theory: An introduction*. New York University Press.

Denner, J., Meyer, B., & Bean, S. (2005). Young women's leadership alliance: Youth – Adult partnerships in an all-female after-school program. *Journal of Community Psychology, 33*(1), 87–100. https://doi-org.ezproxyles.flo.org/10.1002/jcop.20036

Dugan, J. P. (2017). *Leadership theory: Cultivating critical perspectives*. Jossey-Bass.

Edell, D., Brown, L. M., & Tolman, D. (2013). Embodying sexualization: When theory meets practice in intergenerational feminist activism. *Feminist Theory, 14*(3), 275–285. https://doi.org/10.1177/1464700113499844

Gammel, J. A., Motulsky, S. L., & Rutstein-Riley, A. (2017). Relational mentoring: Connection, mutuality, and empowerment. In *Mapping the field of adult and continuing education*. Routledge.

Girl Scout Research Institute. (2008). *Change it up! What girls say about redefining leadership*. Girl Scouts of the USA. https://www.girlscouts.org/content/dam/girlscouts-gsusa/forms-and-documents/about-girl-scouts/research/change_it_up_executive_summary_english.pdf

Hammer, E. Y., & Giordano, P. J. (2001). Dual-gender team-teaching human sexuality: Pedagogical and practical issues. *Teaching of Psychology, 28*(2), 132–133.

Hill, D. C. (2016). What happened when I invited students to see me? A Black queer professor's reflections on practicing embodied vulnerability in the classroom. *Journal of Lesbian Studies, 21*(4), 432–442. https://doi.org/10.1080/10894160.2016.1165045

Hooks, B. (1994). *Teaching to transgress: Education as the practice of freedom*. Routledge.

Jordan, J. V. (2018). *Relational cultural therapy* (2nd ed.). American Psychological Association.

Jordan, W. J. (2010). Defining equity: Multiple perspectives to analyzing the performance of diverse learners. *Review of Research in Education, 34*(1), 142–178. https://doi.org/10.3102/0091732X09352898

Lazzari, M. M., Caloarossi, L., & Collins, K. S. (2009). Feminists in social work: Where have all the leaders gone? *Affilia, 24*(4), 348–359. https://doi.org/10.1080/10437797.2015.977162

Lerner, R. M., Almerigi, J. B., Theokas, C., & Lerner, J. V. (2005). Positive youth development a view of the issues." *The Journal of Early Adolescence, 25*(10), 10–16. https://doi.org/10.1177/0272431604273211

Lewis, M. G. (1993). *Without a word: Teaching beyond women's silence*. Routledge.

Linkon, S. L. (1992). From experience to analysis: Using student discomfort in the feminist classroom. *Transformations, 3*, 57–67. http://dx.doi.org/10.1177/1350506811426237c

Maher, F. A., & Tetreault, M. (1994). *The feminist classroom*. Basic Books.

McArthur, J. (2015). Assessment for social justice: The role of assessment in achieving social justice. *Assessment & Evaluation in Higher Education, 41*(7), 967–981. https://doi.org/10.1080/02602938.2015.1053429

McCusker, G. (2017). A feminist teacher's account of her attempts to achieve the goals of feminist pedagogy. *Gender and Education, 29*(4): 445–460. https://doi.org/10.1080/09540253.2017.1290220

Mezirow, J., & Associates (Eds.). (1990). *Fostering critical reflection in adulthood*. Jossey-Bass.

Miller, J. B. (1996). *Toward a new psychology of women*. Beacon Press.

Minnich, E. (2005). *Transforming knowledge* (2nd ed.). Temple University Press.

Owen, J. (2020). *We are the leaders we've been waiting for: Women and leadership development in college*. Stylus.

Pereira, M. D. M. (2012). Uncomfortable classrooms: Rethinking the role of student discomfort in feminist teaching. *European Journal of Women's Studies, 19*(1), 128–135. http://dx.doi.org/10.1177/1350506811426237c

Perrier, M., & Withers, D. (2016): An archival feminist pedagogy: Unlearning and objects as affective knowledge companions. *Continuum: Journal of Media & Cultural Studies, 30*(3), pp. 355–366. https://doi.org/10.1080/10304312.2016.1166561

Rutstein-Riley, A., Walker, J., Diamond, A., Bryant, B., & LaFlamme, M. (2013). We're all straight here: Using girls' groups and critical media literacy to explore identity with middle school girls. In K. Harper, Y. Katsulis, V. Lopez, & G. S. Gillis (Eds.), *Girls' Sexualities and the Media*, (pp. 263–283). Peter Lang.

Rutstein-Riley, A., & Ziergiebel, A. M. (2018). Feminist relational practice: Emerging scholars discover the disorienting dilemma of leadership and transformation. *Feminist Teacher*, 28(2–3), 158–176.

Rutstein-Riley, A., & Ziergiebel, A. M. (2020). The work of girlhood: An invitation to examine self and identity. In J. A. Gamel, S. Motulsky, & A. Rutstein-Riley (Eds.), *Identity and lifelong learning in higher education* (pp. 23–38). Information Age Publishing.

Shah, R., & Kopko, K. (2016) Feminist pedagogy and the Socratic method: Partners in the classroom or a disaster waiting to happen? *Higher Education Studies*, *6*(2), pp. 39–49. https://doi.org/10.5539/hes.v6n2p39

Shea, H. D., & Renn, K. A. (2017). Gender and leadership: A call to action. In D. Tillapaugh & P. Haber-Curran (Eds.), *Critical perspectives on gender and student leadership: New directions for student leadership*, 154, 83–94. Jossey-Bass.

Shrewsbury, C. M. (1997). What is feminist pedagogy? *Women's Studies Quarterly*, *25*(1/2), 166–173. http://www.jstor.org/stable/40003432

Stake, J. E., & Hoffmann, F. L. (2000). Putting feminist pedagogy to the test: The experience of women's studies from student and teacher perspectives. *Psychology of Women Quarterly*, *24*, 30–38. http://dx.doi.org/10.1111/j.1471-6402.2000.tb01019.x

Walker, M. U. (2007). *Moral understandings: A feminist study in ethics*. Oxford University Press.

Webb, L. M., Allen, M. W., & Walker, K. L. (2002). Feminist pedagogy: Identifying basic principles. *Academic Exchange*, *6*, 67–72.

Weiner, C., Van Demark, K., Doyle, S., Martinez, J., Walklet, F., & Rutstein-Riley, A. (2020). The girlhood project: Pivoting our model with girls during COVID-19. *Girlhood Studies*, *13*(3), 32–47. Retrieved May 3, 2024, from https://doi.org/10.3167/ghs.2020.130304

Welde, K. D., Foote, N., Hayford, M., & Rosenthal, M. (2013). Team teaching "gender perspectives": A reflection on feminist pedagogy in the interdisciplinary classroom. *Feminist Teacher*, *23*, 105–125. http://dx.doi.org/10.5406/femteacher.23.2.0105

8 Empowered Voices

Charting the Course of Women's Leadership Through LEAD Mastermind Peer-to-Peer Mentoring Group

Jana Roberts and Amy Rutstein-Riley

> *The mastermind gave me an opportunity to fully believe in myself and in my capabilities and future plans. Despite the gender inequality in the world, the Mastermind program showed me that women all over the world are doing amazing things, and it is all possible.*
>
> LEAD Mastermind Group Participant

Journey to Transformation

In the complex tapestry of leadership, women encounter distinctive opportunities and unique challenges as they navigate through personal growth, career transitions, and the perpetual pursuit of balance. This journey is influenced by personal aspirations, societal expectations, and organizational structures, which play a fundamental role in shaping and reshaping their leadership identity.

This chapter delves into the complexities women face as leaders. We will explore how gender norms, biases, stereotypes, and societal expectations influence women's leadership identities. Through the lens of the Leadership, Enrichment, and Development (LEAD) framework (Spadorcia et al., Women and Leadership Conference, 2018, 2019), our discussion continues by demonstrating how peer mentoring groups can effectively support women in navigating their leadership paths. Drawing on the experiences of a LEAD Mastermind group, we will share insights into the inherent value of promoting gender equity, enriching women's leadership journeys, and creating inclusive environments that leverage the strength of women in leadership roles. This chapter also serves as a guide for other organizations, both within and outside of higher education, seeking to implement similar initiatives.

The LEAD Mastermind group traces its origins back to a highly successful LEAD group of female university faculty members. Insights shared at the 2018 and 2019 International Leadership Association (ILA) Women and Leadership Conferences about the LEAD model and the success of the face-to-face group sparked the idea of establishing a LEAD group in a virtual space for women both within and outside higher education. The ILA's Women and Leadership

DOI: 10.4324/9781003057208-8

Peer-to-Peer Mastermind initiative provided the necessary organizational support for the initiative.

The LEAD Mastermind group was founded on three tenets: leveraging collective wisdom, fostering continued engagement through accountability, and embracing the advantages of a flexible yet structured approach. The pivotal role of collective wisdom, drawing from the diverse experiences and insights of each member, is the bedrock of the LEAD Mastermind group. This approach ensures that every contribution enriches the group's collective knowledge and fosters growth. By incorporating accountability mechanisms, the group assists members in staying focused on their personal and professional development goals. Moreover, the LEAD model's inherent flexibility and adaptability make it ideally suited for virtual environments, allowing it to thrive in any setting. This blend of collective insight, accountability, and adaptability underpins the group's success, making it a powerful tool for personal and professional growth.

Mastermind Groups

Mastermind groups, typically comprised of three to six participants, represent a distinct form of peer-to-peer mentoring. These groups are intended to leverage the collective wisdom and extensive experience of all members (Paetow et al., 2018). Originally prominent in the business sector, mastermind groups seek to dismantle hierarchical power dynamics, promoting equality and mutual respect among individuals with similar professional standings or backgrounds (Abramson et al., 2019).

Mastermind groups elevate the problem-solving capabilities of all members by shifting the focus to collaborative solutions. They offer practical, social, and emotional support, creating a strong sense of belonging among participants. The groups are specifically structured to facilitate collective learning and professional development. They leverage participants' diverse expertise and viewpoints to address obstacles, promote knowledge sharing, and nurture personal and professional growth (Paetow et al., 2018).

Navigating Leadership Identity

Leadership identity is a dynamic, multifaceted construct that evolves over time (DeRue & Ashford, 2010; Komives et al., 2009; McCarron et al., 2023; Turner et al., 2018). It encompasses the integration of personal and professional identities at the individual, relational, and collective levels while also aligning with broader societal norms (Odom & Dunn, 2023). Moreover, leadership identity intersects with other social identities, such as gender, race, and ethnicity, all of which can influence one's perceptions and experiences (Tapia-Fuselier & Beatty, 2023). Recognizing and understanding these intersections is essential for a comprehensive approach to leadership development, especially for women (Dixon et al., 2023).

Leadership identity forms through personal and professional experiences, challenges, feedback, and self-reflection. It represents a core component of a leader's professional growth. Developing a strong leadership identity is crucial for enhancing leadership competencies, as it motivates individuals to engage in leadership activities (Kragt & Day, 2020; Zaar et al., 2020).

Women and Leadership Identity Development

For women, developing a leadership identity is a transformative journey that requires resilience and courage to challenge societal norms and embrace individual leadership styles (Byrne, 2023). It is about harmonizing their leadership and female identities in personal and public spheres (Byrne, 2023). This ongoing process helps form a cohesive leadership identity.

Grounded in feminist praxis, the formation of women's leadership identity involves active participation in leadership roles and taking proactive steps to engage in developmental opportunities. Such development includes formal and informal learning, involvement in networks, advocating for organizational changes to promote inclusivity and equality, and challenging traditional structural dynamics.

Organizational culture is crucial in shaping leadership identity. Supportive environments that prioritize gender equity serve to help women explore diverse leadership styles, build confidence, and enhance their skills. Mentorship, coaching, and networking are also crucial for fostering leadership identity among women, providing the guidance and support necessary to navigate the complexities of leadership (Kalbarczyk et al., 2022).

Challenges to Women's Leadership Identity Development

Women in leadership frequently encounter distinct hurdles, often rooted in societal attitudes and cultural norms that valorize masculine traits (Maheshwari & Nayak, 2020). These stereotypes and unsupportive environments can impede how women perceive and enact their leadership roles (Dixon et al., 2023; McKenzie, 2018). Unfortunately, internal conflicts regarding leadership roles and identity can significantly disrupt careers (Blake & Fielding, 2023). The lack of female role models further exacerbates underrepresentation and reinforces gender stereotypes, complicating the formation of a strong leadership identity. Intersectionality adds another layer of complexity, with factors such as race, ethnicity, age, and socioeconomic status influencing each woman's leadership identity.

Balancing professional and personal responsibilities is another significant challenge for women in leadership roles. Elevated self-expectations, dual responsibilities, and entrenched gender norms intensify this struggle (Maheshwari & Nayak, 2020). Societal expectations further complicate matters by promoting the expectation that women should place family over career aspirations. Corporate cultures often perpetuate the stereotype that successful leaders must prioritize professional commitments over personal well-being (Jacob & Chandrasekhar, 2021).

Career Transitions

Many women find career transitions rather complex, involving psychological adjustments and a reassessment of what constitutes career success (Motulsky, 2010). These transitions often involve self-discovery and the redefinition of personal and professional identity. For many women, career success encompasses more than promotions and salary increases; they may prioritize work-life balance, societal contributions, and personal fulfillment. Women's non-linear career paths challenge traditional, linear models. Personal decisions, family responsibilities, societal expectations, and workplace cultures influence these non-linear career paths.

The transition into parenthood marks a significant milestone in many women's lives, profoundly affecting their career paths and personal well-being. This pivotal moment often prompts shifts in both their personal and professional identities, causing potential career disruptions. Studies have shown that parenthood tends to have a pronounced impact on women's careers, causing long-term effects on their employment and earnings (Muller et al., 2020. Furthermore, Elez et al. (2021) highlighted that the career implications of becoming a parent are notably more pronounced for women than for men, affecting their job satisfaction and opportunities for career advancement.

Organizational cultures that are supportive play a significant role in shaping the leadership identity of women, especially during periods of transition. These cultures not only bolster women's effectiveness but also facilitate a better work-life balance and enhance their ability to manage dual demands (Hua et al., 2018; Squires & Peach, 2020). Moreover, organizations that embrace gender-diverse leadership and emphasize the importance of work-life balance see notable benefits such as increased employee performance, higher team productivity, and a boost in their appeal as potential employers (Brue, 2018).

Mentorship as a Catalyst for Leadership Identity Development

Mentorship catalyzes women's leadership identity development. It serves as a foundational element in empowering women as they progress in their careers, navigate challenges, and shape their leadership identities (Barkhuizen et al., 2022). Mentors are instrumental in offering guidance on work-life balance, managing responsibilities, and preventing burnout. It is essential for mentors not only to recognize but also to validate the leadership potential of women (Brue & Brue, 2018). By acting as role models, female mentors help build other women's confidence, bolster their self-efficacy, and create a strong support network. Through mentorship, women can establish meaningful professional and personal connections, helping to reduce the sense of isolation often experienced due to underrepresentation in leadership positions (Joseph & McKenzie, 2022).

Sponsorship further empowers women leaders by increasing their visibility and credibility, broadening their professional networks, bridging career gaps, and promoting upward mobility (Gottlieb & Travis, 2018; Singh & Vanka, 2020). Coaching complements these efforts by helping women recognize their strengths, address potential areas for improvement, and craft strategic career goals (Batara & Woolgar, 2017; Fox & Champion, 2022; Johnson & Flores, 2021). Networking is another key component in forging a leadership identity by nurturing connections, promoting collaboration, and enabling the exchange of knowledge. Additionally, networking provides access to diverse perspectives and pathways for professional growth.

The combination of mentorship, sponsorship, coaching, and networking creates an inclusive environment that values diverse perspectives. These components further enhance diversity within organizations by nurturing women's leadership identities, thus enhancing an organization's capacity to meet the needs of a diverse workforce and clientele.

The Power of Peer-to-Peer Mentoring

Peer-to-peer mentoring programs have become a powerful tool for empowering women. In these programs, experienced peers offer guidance, support, and knowledge to those who are less experienced. This model also includes reverse mentoring, creating a reciprocal relationship that effectively addresses the unique challenges that women face in professional and academic settings.

One of the critical strengths of peer-to-peer mentoring is its recognition of the gender-specific challenges women encounter. This shared experience fosters empathy and solidarity, allowing for open discussions about gender bias, work-life balance, and career advancement (Biehle et al., 2021; Chesler et al., 2003; Rockinson-Szapkiw et al., 2021). Peer-to-peer mentoring improves women's leadership capabilities and self-confidence while creating support networks and connections to a broader community of peers. Additionally, participation in these groups can amplify career opportunities through collaborations, job opportunities, and the exchange of professional advice.

Beyond meeting immediate professional needs, peer-to-peer mentoring helps enhance women's leadership identity development and prepares them for future leadership roles. Working with mentors in leadership positions provides valuable insights into strategic thinking and decision-making processes. This collaboration cultivates a cohort of female leaders, adept at handling the complexities of senior leadership roles. This effectively diminishes the gender disparities in leadership roles across various sectors.

Feminist Perspectives on Mentorship

Feminist mentoring theories provide a valuable framework for enhancing peer-to-peer mentoring initiatives, empowering women in leadership roles, and addressing systemic gender inequality. These theories stress the importance of connections, address the unique challenges faced by women leaders, and examine power dynamics and intersectionality (Banerjee et al., 2018). This approach allows for a more comprehensive exploration of power structures and intersecting identities, going beyond the confines of traditional mentoring frameworks.

From a feminist perspective, mentorship actively confronts structural barriers and offers personalized psychosocial support (Manongsong & Ghosh, 2023). This holistic method ensures that women receive comprehensive support tailored to their varied life priorities (Sotirin & Goltz, 2023). Embracing this feminist approach to mentoring not only enhances growth opportunities for women in leadership roles but also aids in creating a more equitable and inclusive professional environment.

LEAD Mastermind Peer-to-Peer Mentoring Program

The LEAD Mastermind program leverages a wealth of literature on mentoring, feminist collaborations, and critical feminist analysis to create a peer-to-peer mentoring framework. This approach effectively supports women leaders during key career and life transitions, fostering an environment of empowerment and transformation. At its core is an adaptable structure designed to maximize the benefits of a cohort-based learning experience. This deliberate configuration brings together women from a rich mosaic of backgrounds, career stages, and cultures, encouraging deep exploration and meaningful evolution of leadership identities.

This program is built on the premise that leader identity development requires more than just improving skills. It necessitates a fundamental shift in how participants perceive themselves and their potential roles in their professional lives. By facilitating interactions among peers with diverse yet relatable experiences, the program ensures a rich exchange of ideas, experiences, and challenges specific to women in leadership. These interactions broaden perspectives and establish a robust support system, enabling participants to redefine and fully embrace their leadership identities.

The LEAD Mastermind program transcends traditional mentoring; it sparks profound personal and professional growth. Tapping into the collective wisdom and support of a diverse cohort of women creates an environment that naturally fosters transformative learning. This approach not only enhances individual leadership capabilities but also builds a network of influential female leaders prepared to shape and enrich their respective fields.

Initially established as an in-person initiative at a university, the LEAD Mastermind program has significantly expanded its reach. Transitioning to an online format enabled the program to welcome women from various sectors, industries, and positions, reflecting a deliberate effort to foster a more inclusive and diverse community. This online format ensures that all participants, regardless of location or industry, have access to mentorship opportunities and a supportive network, advancing the program's mission to empower and elevate female leaders worldwide.

This inclusive approach addresses the distinct opportunities and challenges women may encounter in professional environments. By welcoming participants from various fields, such as technology, marketing, consulting, education, and public service, the LEAD Mastermind group benefits from a broad range of perspectives and expertise. Such diversity enhances group discussions and encourages a more comprehensive exchange of ideas and strategies. Women in senior leadership roles, mid-career professionals, and entry-level positions can now come together in this virtual space, each contributing valuable insights and experiences to the group.

The LEAD Mastermind is an intensive eight-month program designed to foster deep engagement and continuous development among its participants. Monthly meetings are thoughtfully structured to maximize interaction and personal growth. Through structured learning, peer support, and self-directed activities, the LEAD Mastermind program provides a comprehensive and transformative experience for female leaders at critical pivot points in their professional journeys.

The program's methodology centers on shared group norms, which were collaboratively established at the beginning of the eight-month experience and revisited at each meeting. These norms guide interactions, ensuring a respectful and supportive environment that encourages open discussion and vulnerability. In a typical LEAD Mastermind group, meetings begin with individual check-ins, allowing participants to share updates and reflect on their progress and challenges since the previous meeting. These check-ins foster accountability and strengthen the support network within the cohort. This practice also ensures that the program remains highly relevant and responsive to the evolving needs of its participants, thereby maximizing its impact.

During each meeting, participants engage in dialogic and self-exploration activities emphasizing collective creativity, peer accountability, and mutual support. These interactions foster deep, meaningful conversations, encouraging participants to set and pursue ambitious goals. This collaborative approach shifts the focus from individual accomplishments to advancing together, creating a shared journey of empowerment and development.

Each session features member-led presentations on topics relevant to women in leadership roles, such as strategic communication, negotiation skills, work-life balance, and overcoming systemic barriers. These presentations tap into the unique expertise and experiences within the group, fostering a greater sense of ownership and engagement.

Following each presentation, structured group discussions are facilitated to encourage participants to reflect on the material, share their own experiences, and collaboratively develop practical applications of the knowledge. This dialogic approach deepens understanding and nurtures a supportive network where members can explore solutions to common challenges and reinforce their learning through peer feedback.

Journal reflections are vital to the LEAD Mastermind program, promoting deeper personal reflection and professional growth. Participants are encouraged to maintain regular journal entries to capture their insights, address challenges, and celebrate breakthroughs. The result is a valuable archive of their growth journey.

Additional reflective activities are strategically included during meetings to further enrich the learning process. These activities, such as guided self-assessment exercises and reflective questioning, prompt participants to think critically about their experiences and the skills they are developing. This deliberate reflection helps reinforce learning, encouraging participants to internalize and apply the concepts discussed in practical, real-world contexts.

These reflective practices are essential for deepening participants' understanding of their leadership styles and taking more purposeful actions in their career paths. They not only enhance the individual learning experience but also strengthen the collective wisdom of the group, fostering a culture of continuous improvement and self-awareness.

The program also incorporates creative exercises to enhance participants' personal and professional development. For instance, vision boards help participants visualize their goals and aspirations, facilitating reflection and synthesis of personal and professional objectives. The leadership path activity also encourages participants to artistically represent their individual leadership journeys, deepening personal insight and fostering shared understanding within the group.

To complement these visual and creative projects, the program integrates selected shared readings aligned with monthly topics designed to provoke thought and stimulate discussion. These readings serve as a springboard for rich dialogue, allowing participants to explore complex leadership issues from diverse perspectives. The interactive nature of these meetings creates a dynamic learning environment that responds to participants' needs and interests, cultivating a culture of continuous learning and mutual support. These sessions also broaden participants' leadership competencies and strengthen their ability to implement effective leadership strategies within their organizations and networks.

Voices of Empowerment: The Participant Experiences

This analysis of the eight-month LEAD Mastermind program explores the personal and professional growth experienced by its participants. This section aims to connect individual narratives to broader thematic concepts, underscoring the program's significant role in shaping and reshaping women's leadership identity.

We're All in This Together

A pivotal aspect of the LEAD Mastermind program is its focus on cultivating a sense of community and mutual support among its participants. This ethos was reflected by one member who shared, "Hearing her story was a game-changer for me . . . it made me see that we're all in this together."

This sense of community and mutual support was a recurring theme, with many participants conveying their appreciation for the personalized advice and steadfast support they received, which were critical for navigating the complexities of their leadership roles. One member highlighted the significance of having a supportive network, noting, "It is important to always have someone guiding you, someone with experience and understanding of the great potential you have which you might not have yet discovered." This illustrates the essential role mentorship plays in uncovering and nurturing hidden talents and instilling confidence.

The program's effectiveness is also attributed to the recognition of the impact members have on one another. One participant reflected, "A pivotal moment for me in the Mastermind group was when I became aware of the effect of my support on younger professionals." This observation emphasizes the importance of creating a space where mutual respect and collective growth are prioritized.

Safe and Inclusive Spaces

The effectiveness of the LEAD model is largely attributed to its capacity to foster a safe and inclusive environment. This is crucial as it allows participants to express vulnerabilities and share personal insights without fear of judgment. Such a nurturing atmosphere not only promotes individual growth but also contributes to collective growth. Reflecting on the value of the LEAD model, one member noted, "The method was very useful as it created a safe space for everyone to share their expectations and ideas." Another participant remarked, "It really helped to create a safe space for us." This sentiment was echoed by numerous participants, highlighting a widespread recognition of the supportive climate created by the LEAD model. These narratives underscore the model's success in creating an environment that encourages open dialogue and mutual respect – essential for engaging in deep, meaningful interactions.

Holistic Support

As participants became more comfortable sharing their experiences and challenges, they became more receptive to insights and feedback from their peers. Within just two meetings, there was a noticeable shift in the group from offering purely professional support to establishing a more holistic approach that also addressed the emotional and social needs of the group members. This evolution underscores the program's adaptability and ability to meet its members' diverse needs. Participants particularly valued this aspect, especially those navigating significant life and career transitions. Reflecting on this shift, one participant observed,

> I am not sure if it qualifies as a significant impact, but something that stands out is how the group morphed from one of a professional support network to also being a social and emotional support system for those dealing with life challenges and career changes.

This observation emphasizes the LEAD Mastermind program's success in creating a supportive environment that addresses the broad spectrum of its participants' needs.

Imposter Syndrome

Another key issue the LEAD Mastermind group tackled was the pervasive challenge of imposter syndrome affecting women in leadership roles. The group offered a supportive environment for members to share their insecurities and overcome feelings of inadequacy openly. One participant shared a poignant moment, "In our Mastermind group, one session really stood out for me. We were discussing how to tackle imposter syndrome . . . and how, with support, we can push past our doubts." This narrative powerfully highlights the model's triumph in creating an atmosphere that fosters community support, thereby enhancing resilience and bolstering self-confidence.

The emphasis of the LEAD model on providing safe and inclusive spaces proved crucial. The testimonials from participants demonstrated the profound impact of feeling supported and secure within the group. This supportive environment allows for a deeper exploration of leadership identities, enhanced by the collective wisdom and support of the mentoring community. This underscores the model's effectiveness in shaping an environment conducive to learning and growth.

Views on Leadership

The shared experiences within the program bolstered the participants' confidence in their leadership capacities. One participant explained, "Being part of this group has made me more confident as a leader." The program also profoundly reshaped participants' views on leadership, steering them away from traditional authoritative models to a more inclusive and collaborative approach. This shift reflects a more significant trend toward embracing leadership paradigms prioritizing diversity, collective strength, and shared decision-making. For instance, one participant shared, "Being part of the program has really shifted how I approach my work. I've learned so much about the value of different perspectives."

Participants deepened their understanding of these dynamic leadership frameworks and began applying them in their professional settings. "Since joining the Mastermind group, I've really come to see leadership differently – it's much more about collaboration than I used to think," one participant observed, underscoring the program's impact on their leadership philosophy and style. This transformation was especially evident in conversations where blending diverse viewpoints resulted in innovative solutions and strategies, underscoring the advantages of working collaboratively.

Additionally, the program validated pre-existing beliefs about the obstacles to leadership, particularly for women in male-dominated fields. This revelation is significant because it sheds light on the persistent challenges that female leaders face. The insights gained led participants to reevaluate their career trajectories and champion systemic change. By acknowledging and tackling these systemic issues, the group empowered its members to face potential difficulties head-on, providing them with essential knowledge and tactics to overcome these hurdles successfully.

Leadership and Followership

Participants also viewed leadership as a dynamic journey of growth and adaptation. As one participant expressed, "You are never too young or too old to make change and be impactful. You are never too experienced either, so you learn every day from everyone around you." These statements underscore the dynamic nature of leadership, emphasizing that every interaction and challenge offers an opportunity for growth, regardless of where one finds themselves in their professional journey.

Decision-Making

Participants integrated elements from the LEAD Mastermind group into everyday decision-making. Many group members relied on the collective wisdom and counsel from the group as standards for their professional choices, showcasing the profound influence of the LEAD Mastermind on strategic thinking. One participant said, "It has been working as guidance for my day-to-day life. Like a reference book in certain situations where I find myself stuck, I often ask myself what X would do or what would she have said to you at this moment?" Another participant remarked, "There will always be obstacles. If I don't address a difficulty now, it's likely to resurface later in life. Approach everything with courage and confront it with determination." Insights gained by the participants became indispensable to their decision-making repertoire, expanding their ability to navigate complex challenges more confidently.

Leadership Goals

The program had a lasting impact on participants, beyond solving immediate issues to shaping future career plans and aspirations. Through group discussions and self-reflection, participants revisited their long-term goals, realigning them with their personal and professional values.

Their stories vividly illustrated their aspirations and envisioned paths, demonstrating the profound influence of the program. One participant, deeply inspired by the nurturing and growth-oriented environment, shared her future vision: "In 5–10 years, I see myself occupying leadership roles in human rights spaces. Supporting in making the voices of the most vulnerable women and children to be heard and supported."

Another participant expressed a similarly ambitious vision fueled by the confidence and strategic insight developed through the Mastermind program. They stated, "In 5–10 years, I aim to be in a senior leadership role, shaping policy and strategy." This goal is a testament to the program's success in nurturing individual leadership capabilities and motivating participants to apply these skills at higher organizational and societal levels.

The interconnected themes that emerged demonstrate that the essence of leadership identity transcends mere holding of a position of power. Leadership identity encompasses the continuous process of self-exploration, the power of collective encouragement, and the transformative impact of mentorship. These components work together to forge a robust and authentic identity powered by a deep understanding of one's influence within a community of peers. This development not only empowers individual leaders but also enhances the group's collective strength, fostering a dynamic and supportive leadership environment.

Leadership Identity Development

The LEAD Mastermind program and similar initiatives promote the development of women's leadership identity in several ways. First, they create safe and inclusive spaces where women can share their experiences, successes, and challenges without fear of judgment. By sharing and learning from the group's collective wisdom, women are empowered to see beyond their individual challenges, fostering a sense of solidarity and shared purpose. As a result, participants become more confident in their leadership abilities and feel a reinforced sense of belonging and legitimacy as leaders.

At the heart of these initiatives is holistic support, crucial in addressing the complex dimensions of women's lives. This includes offering professional advice and emotional backing, ensuring a well-rounded approach to help women adeptly manage the delicate balance between their personal and professional obligations. This holistic approach, in turn, fosters a stronger sense of leadership identity. Additionally, these programs provide a platform for open discussions about feelings of inadequacy, empowering women to conquer imposter syndrome. Hearing from peers who share similar experiences not only validates their challenges and accomplishments but also enhances their belief in their own abilities, further boosting their self-efficacy and solidifying their leadership identity.

The reflective practices built into the LEAD Mastermind program also encourage deep personal insight and continuous improvement. Participants can incorporate their experiences into their evolving leadership identities by engaging in activities such as discussions and journaling. The program's emphasis on strategic goal setting and visioning also helps women articulate and pursue ambitious career aspirations. Aligning their leadership identity with long-term goals enables participants to better navigate their professional journeys with greater purpose and resilience.

Furthermore, exposure to different perspectives and collaborative problem-solving, fundamental to the LEAD program, shifts participants' views towards more inclusive and collective leadership styles. This improves their strategic thinking and decision-making skills and aligns their leadership practices with contemporary, effective leadership paradigms.

Initiatives such as the LEAD Mastermind group profoundly shape women's leadership identities by providing a supportive, inclusive, and reflective environment that nurtures personal and professional growth, combats imposter syndrome, and encourages collaborative leadership practices.

Envisioning the Future

As we envision the future, the transformative power of initiatives such as the LEAD Mastermind program becomes increasingly evident. These initiatives extend far beyond providing a space for women to gather, share opportunities, and tackle challenges. They are about reshaping leadership paradigms, fostering inclusive environments, and dismantling the systemic barriers that hinder women's progress. At the heart of their effectiveness is the cultivation of a strong leadership identity, empowering women to embrace and embody their leadership roles with confidence.

The future of leadership will be shaped by the courageous, resilient, and empowered women who emerge from these mentoring programs. By continuing to invest in and expand initiatives such as the LEAD Mastermind, we can ensure that more women can access the support and resources needed to succeed. These programs are poised to nurture a new generation of leaders who are not only equipped with critical leadership skills and knowledge but also deeply attuned to their authentic selves and committed to enacting meaningful change.

As we look forward, let us commit to fostering and supporting these programs. Let us envision a future where every woman can realize her full leadership potential, where her journey is honored, and where her impact is profound. The LEAD Mastermind program paves the way for a brighter, more inclusive future where women's leadership is not only supported but celebrated. Together, we can create a legacy for women leaders who will inspire, innovate, and transform the world.

References

Abramson, E. L., Naifeh, M., Stevenson, M. D., & Li, S. T. (2019). Scholarly collaboration, mentorship, and friendship: A new model for success in academic medicine. *Academic Pediatrics*, *19*(8), 860–864. https://doi.org/10.1016/j.acap.2019.07.010

Banerjee, R., Reio, T. G., & Rocco, T. S. (2018). Mentoring functions and outcomes: An integrative literature review of sociocultural factors and individual differences. *Human Resource Development Review*, *18*(1), 114–162. https;//doi.org/10.1177/1534484318810267

Barkhuizen, E. N., Masakane, G., & Lidewey E C van der, S. (2022). In search of factors that hinder the career advancement of women to senior leadership positions. *Sa Journal of Industrial Psychology*, *48*. https://doi.org/10.4102/sajip.v48i0.1986

Batara, N., & Woolgar, T. (2017). The mentorship imperative for health leadership. *Healthcare Management Forum*, *30*(3), 155–158. https://doi.org/10.1177/0840470417692335

Biehle, L., Crowl, A., Park, H. C., Vos, S. S., & Franks, A. M. (2021). The power of peer mentoring to support women pharmacy faculty personally and professionally. *American Journal of Pharmaceutical Education*, *85*(2), 8471. https://doi.org/10.5688/ajpe8471

Blake, C., & Fielding, M. (2023). The mentoring needs of recently appointed female middle leaders: An Australian case study. *International Journal of Mentoring and Coaching in Education*, *12*(3), 316–332. https://doi.org/10.1108/ijmce-06-2022-0045

Brue, K. L. (2018). Harmony and help: Recognizing the impact of work-life balance for women leaders. *Journal of Leadership Education*, *17*(4), 219–243. https://doi.org/10.12806/v17/i4/c2

Brue, K. L., & Brue, S. A. (2018). Leadership role identity construction in women's leadership development programs. *Journal of Leadership Education*, *17*(1), 7–27. https://doi.org/10.12806/v17/i1/c2

Byrne, A. E. (2023). How women leaders' identities coexist through public and private identity endorsements. *Journal of Leadership & Organizational Studies*, *31*(1), 59–75. https://doi.org/10.1177/15480518231208576

Chesler, N. C., Single, P. B., & Mikic, B. (2003). On belay: Peer-Mentoring and adventure education for women faculty in engineering. *Journal of Engineering Education*, *92*(3), 257–262. https://doi.org/10.1002/j.2168-9830.2003.tb00766.x

DeRue, D. S., & Ashford, S. J. (2010). Who will lead and who will follow? A social process of leadership identity construction in organizations. *The Academy of Management Review*, *35*(4), 627–647. https://doi.org/10.5465/AMR.2010.53503267

Dixon, S., Niewoehner-Green, J., Smulowitz, S., Smith, D. N., Rutstein-Riley, A., & Thomas, T. (2023). Girls' and young women's leader identity development: A scoping review. *Gender in Management an International Journal*, *38*(7), 896–924. https://doi.org/10.1108/gm-03-2022-0108

Elez, E., Ayala, F. J., Felip, E., Campelo, R. G., Garcia-Carbonero, R., Donas, J. G., Alba, A. G. D., Flores, E. G., Hidalgo, J., Isla, D., Majem, M., Lescure, Á. R., Safont, M., Santaballa, A., Villacampa, G., Vera, R., & Garrido, P. (2021). Gender influence on work satisfaction and leadership for medical oncologists: A survey of the Spanish Society of Medical Oncology (SEOM). *Esmo Open*, *6*(2), 100048. https://doi.org/10.1016/j.esmoop.2021.100048

Fox, I., & Champion, J. D. (2022). A qualitative thematic analysis of mentorship for new psychiatric-mental health nurse practitioners. *Journal of the American Association of Nurse Practitioners*, *34*(12), 1289–1299. https://doi.org/10.1097/jxx.0000000000000794

Gottlieb, A. S., & Travis, E. L. (2018). Rationale and models for career advancement sponsorship in academic medicine: The time is here; the time is now. *Academic Medicine*, *93*(11), 1620–1623. https://doi.org/10.1097/acm.0000000000002342

Hua, D. W., Mahmood, N. H. N., Zakaria, W. N. W., Lin, L., & Xia, Y. (2018). The relationship between work-life balance and women leadership performance: The mediation effect of organizational culture. *International Journal of Engineering & Technology*, *7*(4), 8. https://doi.org/10.14419/ijet.v7i4.9.20608

Jacob, N., & Chandrasekhar, S. (2021). Advancing female corporate leadership: A comparative analysis of female versus male leadership behaviour in India. *Millennial Asia*, *14*(2), 260–277. https://doi.org/10.1177/09763996211048988

Johnson, S. J., & Flores, H. (2021). Nurse mentors guide medical assistants up the clinical ladder. *Journal for Nurses in Professional Development*, *37*(4), 231–236. https://doi.org/10.1097/nnd.0000000000000758

Joseph, J., & McKenzie, A. I. (2022). Black women coaches in community: Promising practices for mentorship in Canada. *Frontiers in Sports and Active Living*, *4*. https://doi.org/10.3389/fspor.2022.884239

Kalbarczyk, A., Harrison, M., Chung, E., Glass, N., Genberg, B., Decker, M. R., & Manabe, Y. C. (2022). Supporting women's leadership development in global health through virtual events and near-peer networking. *Annals of Global Health*, *88*(1). https://doi.org/10.5334/aogh.3397

Komives, S. R., Longerbeam, S. D., Mainella, F., Osteen, L., Owen, J. E., & Wagner, W. (2009). Leadership identity development: Challenges in applying a developmental model. *Journal of Leadership Education*, *8*(1), 11–47. https://doi.org/10.12806/V8/I1/TF2

Kragt, D., & Day, D. V. (2020). Predicting leadership competency development and promotion among high-potential executives: The role of leader identity. *Frontiers in Psychology*, *11*. https://doi.org/10.3389/fpsyg.2020.01816

Maheshwari, G., & Nayak, R. (2020). Women leadership in Vietnamese higher education institutions: An exploratory study on barriers and enablers for career enhancement. *Educational Management Administration & Leadership*, *50*(5), 758–775. https://doi.org/10.1177/1741143220945700

Manongsong, A. M., & Ghosh, R. (2023). Living at the intersections of race and gender in diversified mentoring: Experiences of minoritized women leaders in higher education. *Advances in Developing Human Resources*, *25*(4), 247–278. https://doi.org/10.1177/15234223231193317

McCarron, G. P., McKenzie, B. L., & Yamanaka, A. (2023). Leadership identity development. *New Directions for Student Leadership*, *2023*(178), 31–43. https://doi.org/10.1002/yd.20552

McKenzie, B. L. (2018). Am I a leader? Female students' leadership identity development. *Journal of Leadership Education*, *17*(2), 1–18. https://doi.org/10.12806/v17/i2/r1

Motulsky, S. L. (2010). Relational processes in career transition: Extending theory, research, and practice. *The Counseling Psychologist*, *38*(8), 1078–1114. https://doi.org/10.1177/0011000010376415

Muller, J. S., Hiekel, N., & Liefbroer, A. C. (2020). The long-term costs of family trajectories: Women's later-life employment and earnings across Europe. *Demography*, *57*(3), 1007–1034. https://doi.org/10.1007/s13524-020-00874-8

Odom, S. F., & Dunn, A. L. (2023). Leadership identity development in curricular settings. *New Directions for Student Leadership*, *2023*(178), 87–98. https://doi.org/10.1002/yd.20557

Paetow, G., Zaver, F., Gottlieb, M., Chan, T. M., Lin, M., & Gisondi, M. A. (2018). Online mastermind groups: A non-hierarchical mentorship model for professional development. *Cureus*. https://doi.org/10.7759/cureus.3013

Rockinson-Szapkiw, A., Watson, J. H., Gishbaugher, J., & Wendt, J. L. (2021). A case for a virtual STEM peer-mentoring experience for racial and ethnic minority women mentees. *International Journal of Mentoring and Coaching in Education*, *10*(3), 267–283. https://doi.org/10.1108/ijmce-08-2020-0053

Singh, S., & Vanka, S. (2020). Mentoring is essential but not sufficient: Sponsor women for leadership roles. *Development in Learning Organizations an International Journal*, *34*(6), 25–28. https://doi.org/10.1108/dlo-05-2019-0100

Sotirin, P., & Goltz, S. M. (2023). Mid-career faculty peer mentoring: Rationale and program design. *New Directions for Higher Education*, *2023*(201–202), 5–19. https://doi.org/10.1002/he.20467

Spadorcia, S., Rutstein-Riley, A., & Direiter, D. (2017). *Leadership Development for Women Faculty*. 3rd Biennial International Leadership Association Women and Leadership Conference. Rhinebeck, NY, USA.

Squires, E. C., & Peach, J. M. (2020). Effective military leadership: Balancing competing demands. *Canadian Journal of Behavioural Science/Revue Canadienne Des Sciences Du Comportement*, *52*(4), 314–323. https://doi.org/10.1037/cbs0000179

Tapia-Fuselier, N., & Beatty, C. C. (2023). Social identities and leadership identity development. *New Directions for Student Leadership*, *2023*(178), 45–54. https://doi.org/10.1002/yd.20553

Turner, J. R., Baker, R., Schroeder, J., Johnson, K. R., & Chung, C. (2018). Leadership development techniques. *European Journal of Training and Development*, *42*(9), 538–557. https://doi.org/10.1108/EJTD-03-2018-0022

Zaar, S., Bossche, P. V. D., & Gijselaers, W. (2020). How business students think about leadership: A qualitative study on leader identity and meaning-making. *Academy of Management Learning and Education*, *19*(2), 168–191. https://doi.org/10.5465/amle.2017.0290

9 Epilogue

The Kitchen Table

Diana C. Direiter

Early in this project, the editors were deeply inspired by the title and theme of "#Do Power Differently," a women's leadership immersion series at Omega Women's Leadership Center. Regardless of our commitment to doing power differently, however, we still lived and worked in systems that did not necessarily share our philosophy. We endured many of the same minor slights and major struggles as other women, academics, and women academics. There is often a fluidity to leadership within higher education as we might flow from faculty to administration and back again. Each transition necessitates a recalibration of expectations – our own and those around us. When there is just one woman – or very few – in a leadership position, she is an easily identified target (Morgenroth et al., 2020).

Though not specific to females of the species, the concept of reindeer cyclones was highly relevant to our group. It is a defensive strategy in which the stronger reindeer of the herd run as a collective around those more vulnerable who remain protected in the middle. The technique confuses predators and makes it difficult for them to target one reindeer (Espmark & Kinderås, 2002). As leaders in higher education, many of the authors of this book had a turn as the vulnerable member of the "herd." The strategic cyclone of the other LEAD members repeatedly offered invaluable protection.

In the animal world, there are various species in which female leadership is advantageous for the full swarm, pack, or herd. Honeybees, lemurs, elephants, spotted hyenas, bonobos, and orca (aka killer) whales benefit from the females' strengths in communication, finding and sharing resources, and managing between- and within-group conflicts (Smith et al., 2020). LEAD strove to foster a space in which our members felt a sense of ownership of the group – a true collaboration in which the power was diffused across the collective. We have held tight to the belief that even a handful of LEAD-ers doing power differently within a community could benefit the overall organization. Over the time of working on this book, our personal and professional lives changed. We mourned the losses of parents and marriages; we celebrated new relationships, our children's milestones, and the births of grandchildren. We've shared one

DOI: 10.4324/9781003057208-9

another's personal and professional heartaches, disappointments, joys, and successes. Some members of our original group have since left Lesley University for other institutions, and many – including several authors of this book – have retired.

Higher Education has changed, and since LEAD began in 2015, our home university has navigated the transitions of three official presidents and one interim president, as well as three official provosts and three interim provosts.

This book, too, has evolved throughout the years. We had creative ideas that never came to fruition and serendipitous accidents that shifted our focus in a better direction.

As reflexive practitioners, educators, and scholars, we periodically carve out time to reflect together on LEAD. Eight years after LEAD's inception, the authors and editors of *Invitation to LEAD* gathered via Zoom for a "Kitchen Table conversation." We had planned to then analyze this conversation for themes that could then support other elements of the book. Structured by the five questions below, we reflected on our leadership identities and the ways our involvement with LEAD affected our journeys as individuals and as a collective.

- How has LEAD provided a context for each of us, individually as well as us, collectively, to evolve in terms of our internal view of self as a leader, leader, and identity?
- When you look back at your time with LEAD, what moment or moments best capture the memory of it?
- Now it's 2023. Looking forward, what will be on your map next?
- What could you have benefited from us bringing into this space that we hadn't had as part of the LEAD experience together?
- Thinking forward, where do we think this work can be positioned?

It quickly became apparent that this conversation would not actually result in succinct vignettes that crisply illustrated a particular concept. Instead, and more characteristically of the group, the transcription had pages of us laughing, talking over one another, reliving frustrations, recalling special moments, affirming each other's comments, and spontaneous expressions of love and appreciation for one another.

We considered untangling the threads of our kitchen table conversation and then re-weaving them into epigraphs to connect the chapters. We came to realize, however, that the conversation is, itself, emblematic of the LEAD experience. The strength, the power, and the *effectiveness* of the model come not from techniques that can be rewritten into standard operating procedures. It comes, instead, from the inextricability of our perspectives, experiences, and relationships. There is a relational Gestalt that is diluted when disassembled and examined as separate components.

Nevertheless, there were some concepts that surfaced for many of us:

- Our experiences when we were not in a leadership position informed our priorities around communication, collaboration, and connection once we were
- We didn't always recognize our own potential for leadership until we looked through the lenses of our LEAD colleagues
- An understanding that courage is needed for vulnerable leadership
- There is a delicate balance between devotion to our careers and depletion of other parts of our lives
- The effects – both positive and negative – that aging as women have had on our leadership trajectories
- That self-doubt, loneliness, and ambivalence can accompany leadership opportunities

Ultimately, the centerpiece of our kitchen table conversation was the repeated realization of how our leadership voices were tuned within and amplified by our experience with LEAD. Some of the chairs at our table sit empty but serve as a reminder of the contributions of all LEAD-ers who have joined us since we began. Some may have popped in for the equivalent of a quick coffee, while others stayed with us for several courses, but each added an irreplaceable richness to our shared experience. We remain forever grateful to those who have made room at the table over the years and to everyone who accepted our invitation to LEAD.

References

Espmark, Y., & Kinderås, K. (2002). Behavioural lateralisation in reindeer. *Rangifer*, *22*(1), 51–59. https://doi.org/10.7557/2.22.1.687

Morgenroth, T., Kirby, T. A., Ryan, M. K., & Sudkämper, A. (2020). The who, when, and why of the glass cliff phenomenon: A meta-analysis of appointments to precarious leadership positions. *Psychological Bulletin*, *146*(9), 797–829. https://doi-org.ezproxyles.flo.org/10.1037/bul0000234

Smith, J. E., Ortiz, C. A., Buhbe, M. T., & van Vugt, M. (2020). Obstacles and opportunities for female leadership in mammalian societies: A comparative perspective. *The Leadership Quarterly*, *31*(2). https://doi.org/10.1016/j.leaqua.2018.09.005

Index

Note: Page numbers in italic indicate a figure, and page numbers in bold indicate a table on the corresponding page.